INSIDE A COP

Tensions
in the
Public and Private Lives
of the Police

Roger Baldwin

THE BOXWOOD PRESS

ISBN: 0-910286-55-8

Distributed by:

THE BOXWOOD PRESS
183 Ocean View Blvd.
Pacific Grove, CA 93950

408—375-9110

Cover photo by Audrey C. Tiernan

Printed in U.S.A.

CONTENTS

PREFACE

It is difficult, perhaps futile and entirely useless, to know who the first one was to kindle the spark that fired an author to produce a book. I find myself no exception in this regard. Yet, I have clear memories of Bob Swab, formerly a Police Services Consultant for the Pennsylvania Department of Public Instruction, suggesting that a book such as *Inside a Cop* was needed and that I should write it. I really don't remember whether he, Cecil Yates, or Fred Miller, of that department (now part of the Department of Community Affairs), prodded me first. I do recall that Gerry Monahan, when he was Public Safety Director for the City of Allentown, Pa., was the first to "bare" his police department to my scrutiny, as did several chiefs and commissioners. Ralph Kressley, and later Carson Gable (Allentown's current Chief of Police), continued to make my studies possible, especially through the use of their academy, where officers from the entire northeastern section of the state are trained. Bob Galle, the commissioner of the Bethelehem, Pa., Police Department, has rendered invaluable assistance. Whether it was in providing the entire department as subjects or in gathering photos, no one was more courteous or considerate. Since several hundred people participated in some way, most of them police, a list covering almost as many pages as the book itself would be needed to cite them all. Each officer who recognizes himself or herself in some way depicted in the composites developed in the book shares in my gratitude.

Not all of those who urged this book on were police officers. How many times did I hear Ed Sagarin, past president of the American Society of Criminology, say, "Roger, when are you going to put a book together on the police?" And, when I began to write, his criticisms were pointed but encouraging. Richard

Quinney's very positive remarks about the chapters he read were just what I needed to continue. Both his many books and his friendship have been inspirational. Milt Pollen, director of the Justice Administration Program at Lehigh County Community College, also contributed greatly by reading and commenting on chapters of the book.

I would be remiss if I did not mention colleagues and friends such as Fred Smith of Wyomissing High School and Nelvin Vos of Muhlenberg College who read and edited some of the earlier drafts of some chapters. And who could get along without a secretary who never grows impatient as she is asked to type chapters and letters on the spur of the moment? Esther Zotter is that kind of secretary.

It must be clearly stated at the outset that the aid and encouragement received from the many people cited does not necessarily indicate that any of the ideas printed within this book are in any way their responsibility. I did try to reflect in my Eastern City studies the attitudes and ideas of the many officers interviewed and observed, but the final interpretation is wholly my own.

In the incubation period and in the initial years of research and writing, each of my sons—Dennis, John, Steve, and Tim—proudly urged me on. On the twilight side of the book, my daughters—Stephanie, Priscilla, and Hope—each poured life and vitality into Dad. My vibrant, exciting, motivation builder and partner in life, Carol, has been a partner in the development and completion of this work, and it is to her that I dedicate *Inside a Cop*.

Roger Baldwin

Chapter 1

PORTRAIT OF THE POLICE

Just at that moment, the rear of a motorcycle and a side-car carrying three policemen in huge sheepskin coats appeared out of the snowy greyness of the road immediately ahead. It was travelling very slowly, no more than twenty meters in front of us, and we were bearing down on it quickly. "Careful Nadya! I don't suppose you want to crash into the police, of all people?"

She applied the brakes heavily and chuckled, "Why not? If you have to run into someone, they're the best people. Nobody likes those layabouts. We call *musor* [garbage].... And what about over there in the West? Does everybody love the police like they're supposed to?"

"Hardly."

"Of course not, I just asked. People are the same everywhere, after all; nobody likes to be pushed around and lectured to by a puffed up turkey-cock in a blue uniform."[1]

IN RECENT YEARS, national and even international attention has been paid to the subject of the police. The historian of the development of police services would surely note that concern with police departments and their problems and organization can be traced through centuries. In the 16th and 17th centuries in London, for instance, the citizens dubbed as "Charlies" the watchmen who were the forerunners of the modern police. "It was a common sport of rich young men of the time to taunt and terrorize them, to wreck their watch-houses and occasionally to murder them."[2] But one factor separates the current interest in the police from earlier times.

1

The communications media, especially with the advent of television, which has recently widened in scope through satellite transmissions, have extended what might in the recent past have been a critical or important *local* news event into an event of *national* or *international* interest. Although there may be a degree of localism or provincialism among the residents of Boston, New York, Des Moines, or Grand Rapids, when a mine caves in in West Virginia, or the lettuce growers strike in California, or a "rock group" arrives in Philadelphia from England, everyone is sufficiently cosmopolitan to be at least casually aware of these events. The events just do not go unnoticed. It is not only the behavior of the police at national conventions that returns to the public through TV, the press, radio, and magazines. Charges of bribery, conspiracy, and misfeasance and malfeasance in office of the small town chief of police make the news, too.[3].

As if news presentations about police were not enough, popularizing of policemen and policewomen in dramatic series has placed them in the forefront of television fare. It is not unusual to be able to view one or more police programs per night (depending upon the number of channels available in a particular locality). Unfortunately, as one policewoman recently commented, the police serials on television are escape material and nobody takes them any more seriously than they do cartoons.

Nadya's cry of *musor* has its counterpart in the United States, as does the 17th century Londoner's cry of "Charlie," in the battle cry of the youth during the "turbulent sixties," "pig!" The policeman is the most visible public employee who is involved in restricting or regulating the behavior of the same public which employs him. The performance of his duties is always carried out either in public view or in direct interaction with the public. The restrictive and regulative nature of his duties frequently evokes hostility regardless of the personal characteristics of the officer performing them.

The policeman is the sore thumb on the administrative hand of the body politic of society. Because he is highly visible, he cannot—nor does he desire to—be ignored. He is called upon to act in times of trouble and, if he does, he is praised by some and censured by others. If he doesn't act, the same results, praise or censure, occur. These conditions cannot help but produce a confused policeman. Solutions to his dilemma are pouring in from all sides which, instead of rectifying a problematic situation, only heighten the strain and increase the visibility of the policeman. His (or her) cry for equal status with others in the community with a request for equal pay has been met in recent months with threats to lay off members of the department to maintain the local economically tight budget.

Who is the policeman (or policewoman) and what is he (or she) like? How does he see himself? What does he think the public thinks of him? What do his family and friends think of him? What do offenders think of him? What does he consider his appropriate spheres of operations and his potential for carrying out the activities within them effectively? And lastly, what are the limitations imposed by himself and by society upon his behavior which help or hamper him in carrying out the roles of his position? *Inside a Cop* examines these questions and more.

The image held by others cannot help but affect the police officer's performance in his/her duties; self-image is affected by it, and actions reflect it. Yet, up to now, relatively little is known about the police officer as an individual. It is assumed that an officer represents a closed society which sometimes appears to be and reacts as a minority group. With little more detailed knowledge or speculation than this, strong opinions about an officer are expressed—motivations and actions are assumed on the basis of surface impressions. What are the factors which actually precipitate the behavior that is admired by some and detested by others? Why is there such a discrepancy in response? What is the police officer really like?

The studies and observations presented in this book began as an outgrowth of the author's contact with police departments in the role of a part-time instructor in the subject of "juvenile delinquency" in the 1960s. During the ensuing years, the now famous or infamous ghetto riots, political-convention riots, and the "busting" of "hippies" and other youth groups have occurred. Rapidly, the teaching sessions turned away from discussions of juvenile delinquency to the even more pressing subject of riots and the place of the police in them, and eventually to the image of the police held by others and by themselves. This required research on a larger scale than the casual perusal of an occasional article. Much has been done with public opinion but little with the police officers' views of themselves and of others.

Safety-patrol skating party. Police are expected to be "big," "brave," and "fearless," always chasing the "bad guys." They are also expected to be the "jolly-daddy type" with the neighborhood kids. Most officers do one or two well. Few do all effectively. (Bethlehem Police Dept., Bethlehem, Pa.)

Reading newspaper accounts of police activity in New York, Chicago, Los Angeles, and other large metropolitan areas and then forming opinions of the police all over the nation is akin to saying that backyard, sandlot, school, and semi-pro baseball are the same as big league, professional baseball. A good or a bad game can be had in any of these levels, and there is no trouble in recognizing the activity for what it is—from sandlot to pro. Yet, the setting, the various qualifications for membership, and the manner in which the game is performed can differ greatly. If there is an average-size police force, it is not one of 35,653, 14,935, or 10, 137.[4] It is more likely to range from a few to several hundred men. A force of approximately 175 men is more representative of police departments in the majority of urban areas in the United States than one ranging in the thousands, and the slightly more than 35,000 people in New York City's police department constitute a larger group than the population of the majority of small towns in America.

This book was conceived with the idea that the nation's police, who are now thought of in light of the few large forces, could be better known through an in-depth study of a single police force of less than 200 men and women.* It is certainly true that varying size, regional differences, local politics, and other factors make each small force different. Nevertheless, they must share more attributes with each other than with the larger forces which now represent them in the TV and press reports.

When the public becomes aware of a police scandal in New York City or hears about the Knapp Commission, whose function it was to investigate the activities of the New York City Police Department, it quickly generalizes that all police departments are involved in scandal and that all should be investigated. New York City is then taken as representative. Authors of studies of large cities carefully inform their readers of the scope of their studies and the limitations imposed upon the data by the methods used

---

*There are 3 policewomen in the study-area at the time of this writing.

and the resultant limitations on generalizations. Nevertheless, there is little to stop the reader from making whatever assumptions he may make. He has no other body of information from which to generalize. Just as we needed studies such as *Small Town in Mass Society, Suburbia* and *The Levittowners* to tell us what was happening to life outside the big city a decade ago when small towns were proliferating, we need studies of average-sized police departments to tell us of their operations.[5]

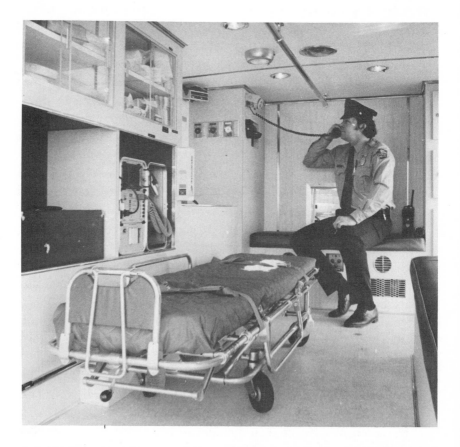

Preparing the cardiac-emergency ambulance for duty. The major portion of the officer's time on duty is spent in meeting a wide variety of community needs. Ambulance work is more common than "shoot-outs." (Call-Chronicle Newspapers, Allentown, Pa.)

It is more likely that the study of the urban police officer in a medium-sized city is representative of the "average" police officer in the United States than the police officer described in national studies or in current thriller-type novels and TV shows. Yet, the reader is cautioned in this book, too, that the content has regional, local, and research biases which limit its utility for generalizations. After all, an image or impression of a subject is never an exact replica. Additionally, in order to assure anonymity while cross-checking the reliability of the data obtained, other nearby communities were from time to time studied, and a composite rather than a picture of a single department was developed.

Little was available in the late 1960s about what any group of police officers had to say about itself except in defense of behavior in riots or other explosive situations. In order to present at least some scant information on group opinion, the officers of Eastern City (the name used throughout the book to denote the composite city described above) were asked two brief, open-ended questions, which left room for either brief or lengthy responses. They asked why some people thought the police are "just great" and others "thought they are not." A serendipitous result was that a number of the officers were very enthusiastic about the exercise and asked that the project be expanded. By 1969, the author was engaged in a study of the attitudes of ex-convicts toward the police. One of the the results of that study was to bring into awareness the fact that the police officers' answers to the questions asked of them the year before reflected a simplistic and somewhat erroneous view of what others think of them. This result reaffirmed the need for a wider look at the police image.

The project began in earnest during the spring of 1970, and by the summer, a pretested set of open-ended questions, a background-information form, an open-ended questionnaire for police officers, one for their spouses, and one for their children over the age of 13 (13 was arbitrarily chosen) were drawn up. During the summer that followed and on and off through the following summers, the author interviewed police officers, spouses, and children.

The material has been continuously updated by re-interviewing.

Only those officers who volunteered to be interviewed in response to a letter (approved of by the police administration but not sponsored by them) were seen. They, in turn, were given the option of having the researcher contact their spouses for this study. The mothers were given a similar option with regard to their children. Clearly, it can be seen that in addition to the fact that some officers might not be married or have children over the age of 13, at each level of option the number of respondents would dwindle. Actually, only 15 children were interviewed, and little can be said directly about police officers' children. However, responses from the officers and their spouses do include data about the officer's relationship with his/her children, and that facet of the police image was developed.

All of the officers, their spouses, and children were invited to be interviewed at the author's office at a nearby college. With the exception of a few wives who were interviewed at their home, the majority of interviews was conducted individually at the college office. (Several of the men wanted to sit in on their wives' interview but were not allowed. They remained in the outer office, which may or may not have influenced the responses of the wives; but this was not noticeable to the interviewer.)

In-depth studies containing open-ended questions administered by a single interviewer leave much to be desired to be scientifically valid. The possibility of replication and identical interpretation of responses is slim. The only minor controls attempted in the 1970-71 study were having the same interviewer for all respondents and the same physical surroundings during most of the interviews. The control is assumed in that the total setting was basically similar for the respondents.

As a police instructor, the author knew most of the officers on familiar terms and assumed that this relationship and their own desire to have the study done gave him greater access to valid responses than would otherwise be available if the study were conducted elsewhere. The men were assured anonymity, which at the time of this writing is even greater in that numerous changes in positions in the departments involved, from patrolman through chief, have occurred.

Over the years that this work has been developing, the author has modified his assumption about relationships with the police and access to valid data. It still appears as though rank-and-file patrolmen are likely to respond truthfully about most matters concerning themselves and their work when they are assured anonymity. They are more relaxed in appearance when discussing family and friends than when discussing work, as one might expect.

The job of a police officer requires that he be suspicious, and he is never without some fear that any negative comments he might make relating to his work may either reach his superiors or make him look less committed to the department and its high, patriotic goals. He is, interestingly enough, much less likely to be frank than the "ex-convict," who will also be discussed in relation to the police image; and he is much more likely to speak freely than the "brass" or command officer.

Policewomen may speak relatively freely either because they have a "freer" attitude or because they are, in this study, in the lower ranks. One woman was hesitant to speak at all without the approval of the chief.

As earlier indicated, ex-convicts were interviewed in a study conducted by the author in 1969. Although they were assured anonymity and were explicitly told that the author did not want to discuss their personal lives with them, that the entire study was to focus upon their contact and relationship with the police, they talked at length about themselves and their lives of crime. Only after they had satisfied the urge to "tell all" were they willing to respond to questions about the police.

The command officers were the most guarded and most sensitive in responding to questions. One of the first commanders to respond to the study began his interview by revealing that many of the command did not want to respond because the form letter sent to them was too impersonal. Friends would have either phoned or written a note in longhand, the author was told. Others were dis-

tressed that the letter noted official approval had been obtained
from the department before the officers were contacted. They
resented that anyone would be involved in their decision to be
interviewed. Even when the author clarified that official approval
was necessary (since they were, in part, discussing the operations

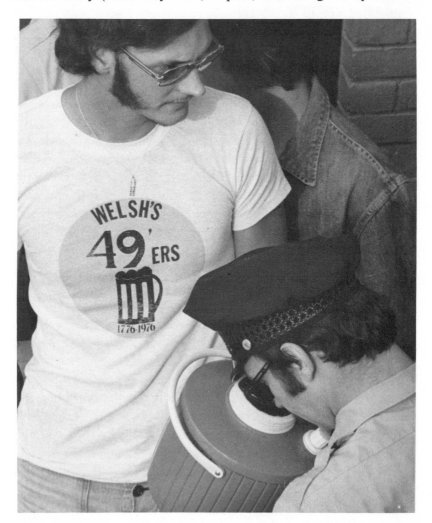

Police dogging dope. Police officers earn no great respect from the crowds of
youth when they search all containers for marijuana and other illegal sub-
stances. (Call-Chronicle Newspapers, Allentown, Pa.)

of a governmental agency which employed them and which was releasing most of them from their official duties during the interviews), some officers reported through others who responded that they felt they were still slighted. As the author's relationship with many of the officers was friendly, none could be described as intimately friendly; and the excuses reported were simply evasionary tactics. If we look at the three categories of respondents— patrol, ex-convicts, and command officers—it becomes clear that those with the least to lose by frank commentary and who spoke frankly were the ex-convicts. Conversely, the command officers with the assumption of the most to lose if quoted directly, were the most evasive.

The responses and the book itself are rounded out with the data obtained from the spouses, children, and from the vice squad, a specialized group of officers. The outstanding characteristics of the wives' responses were the external expressions of support and their resentment toward the department. The vice squad, as a special unit of the department, is presented as an example of the complex decision-making problems faced by such a unit and by other officers, problems magnified by the self-image held by the officer, the changing morality of the times, and the legal boundaries within which the police officer performs.

This book is not intended to be either a dart board for the critics of the police or one for the police themselves. Ironically, the hypercritical will probably react to both positive and neutral statements negatively, and the police will probably do the same with negative and neutral ones. Both groups, therefore, show negativism toward neutral statements. Each side demands the full support of the general public and neither receives it!

During one of several interviews with Captain Brown, the researcher was lectured to at some length on the subject of *the overstudied and overly abused police officer*. The captain began his discourse with the disclosure that at least several times a week [perhaps an exaggeration], various governmental agencies request or demand data and private agencies or organizations want to

Gathering data from the records. Police departments are accustomed to frequent surveillance by governmental agencies and to independent studies by both public and private research agencies. Although cautious and fearful that the data will be used against them, as they sometimes are, police are generally courteous and cooperative. (Robert Reier)

survey some aspect of police work. All demands and requests are met with suspicion.

Most times, data already routinely gathered by the department will suffice for official agencies, and therefore the work of the rank and file membership is not directly interrupted. However, unless the use of the data is clarified, the department remains uncertain of what use may be made of it. Guesses turn to rumors. In most cases, the department eventually learns that little use was made of the data and that the anxiety about it was unwarranted. Still, the apprehension was experienced.

Unofficial studies are greeted with suspicion and hostility because, as Captain Brown noted, "researchers often collect data and then use them against us." Several examples were cited although they were general rather than specific cases. "Researchers," he noted, "cite minimal education or minimal in-service-training as the factors which tend to make Eastern City's Police Department an inferior one." In actuality, based on the crime rate reported in the Uniform Crime Reports as a reflection of police efficiency and effectiveness, Eastern City has little need to feel inferior to other forces of similar size in medium-sized cities. Brown's sensitivity to real or imagined slights reflects a double annoyance—an annoyance with an attack upon the department and an implied attack upon the inadequacy of its individuals. This second annoyance is one to keep in mind throughout any reading of officers' responses to research questions. While seemingly offensive on the street or in the interview, their stance is always defensive.

Despite the general reluctance to participate in research projects, the officers of Eastern City and their superiors do participate. They do so, for the most part, with a cooperative spirit when convinced that the study could potentially aid the department and that the department might indirectly receive benefits from it. The women on the force did not differ from the men; like the men, they showed hesitancy at being interviewed and reflected it by missing the first scheduled interview, as many of the men did. In all cases, both male and female officers knew that they had the approval of the department to participate in the research which is reported in these chapters.

Fewer than 2 percent of those interviewed showed any sustained hostility toward the projects. The reasons for the cooperative attitude of Eastern City's police force were: (1) They were highly suspicious of studies dependent solely upon quantitative data which purport to describe them. The in-depth interviews used most often in these studies are primarily qualitative. (2) They were able to *express their views* and make them publically known to a wide audience without fear of individual repercussions. (3) Lastly, they could in this manner determine individually and without threat t their interpersonal relationships whether their own life experiences and private views coincided with the majority's experiences and views.

Eastern City's police officers, once in 1970 directly before in-depth interviews were held, and again in 1976, responded to a questionnaire about familial and social background. In addition, a second city of similar size with a force of approximately the same number was polled in 1976 to see if Eastern City's self-report appeared to be unique. It was not. Nor was it different when spot checked in several of the characteristics with other police personnel elsewhere.

Since the second decade of this century, the human ecology school of thought in sociology has presented the notion that much can be learned about people and their behavior by examining the spatial locations of their homes, the types of homes in general, and the neighborhoods in which they reside. Upper class people, for example, are not only higher in status socially, economically, and occupationally but are additionally elevated—if the terrain is in any way uneven—by residing higher up the hillside than the other classes. Their life-style is reflected in their physical environment.

Notes

1. An Observer, *Message from Moscow* (New York: Random House, 1971), pp. 176-177.

2. Johnathan Rubinstein, "From the King's Peace to the Patrol Car: The Origins of the City Police," *New York,* May 14, 1973, p. 44.

3. "Judge Drops 3 Charges Chief Faced," *Allentown* (Pa.) *Morning Call,* Sept. 27, 1973, p. 14. The charges dropped against a police chief in a nearby county were blackmail, extortion, and solicitation of a bribe.

4. *Uniform Crime Report 1974.* Police statistics for New York City, Chicago, and Los Angeles.

5. Vidich, Arthur, and Bensman, Joseph, *Small Town in Mass Society* (Princeton, N.J.: Princeton Univ. Press, 1969); Wood, Robert G., *Suburbia* (Boston: Houghton Mifflin, 1959); Gans, Herbert, *The Levittowners* (New York: Pantheon Books, 1967).

Chapter **2**

SOUTH SIDE—DOWNTOWN

NO DOUBT there are those who may take exception to the fact;
but as the late popular songwriter Jim Croce sang it, Big Bad
Leroy Brown came from the *South* Side of Chicago; the school
bussing riots of Boston took place at *Southie* (South Boston High
School); *South* Jamaica in New York City and *South* "Phillie"
(Philadelphia) have long been noted for their gang problems. In
this regard, Eastern City and other cities of its size share with the
larger cities the dubious honor of having "tough" *south* sides
that are also either downtown or on the outskirts of an area designated "downtown."

Eastern City's *south* side is where the greatest number of tough
kids live. From this area come the largest number of those who will
be the future inmates of our jails or prisons and the largest number
of those who will become our city police. Sutherland's theory of
"differential association" or Cloward and Ohlin's "differential
opportunity" theory both explain that those young people who
have the most frequent contact with others who are involved or
who themselves are involved and who have learned the techniques
and developed the motivations toward or away from crime within
their contacts, will most likely turn toward a career in crime or in
law enforcement, depending upon which association or opportunity has been more compelling.[1]

Of Eastern City's police officers, 58 percent grew up on the
south side of town. If one adds to that figure the 12 percent who

16

lived in the area nearest the south side, the east side (which, according to the monthly juvenile unit's zone report, is also a high-delinquency area), an impressive 70 percent of Eastern City's police grew up in its poorest and toughest neighborhoods. Of their fathers, two-thirds were blue collar workers and most of them were laborers. The others worked in factories or as mechanics. The upper third were described as having technical positions with the exception of two who were in management. Their mothers, as one might expect, remained at home as housewives; and if they

The South Side. A factory or two, a railroad station, a water tower, and a Rescue Mission dot the south side of town. It's the tough side, and it's the place where the kids play cops-and-robbers and often grow up to be one or the other. (Robert Reier)

worked, they were employed in unskilled or semi-skilled occupations. Actually, more of the mothers than the fathers had some higher education. Overall, 80 percent of the mothers and 88 percent of the fathers had less than a high school education. The 30 percent of the mothers who were employed were almost all factory workers. The most impressive factor among these cold figures is that 60 percent of the parents of police officers owned their own homes, even under the adverse conditions of the south (and east) side.

The majority (66.6 percent) of Eastern City's police officers grew up in *blue collar* families similar to those described by Mirra Komarovsky 14 years ago.[2] Whatever their ethnic heritage, they were traditional families, hard working, with father the patriarch of the household and mother responsible to maintain that household and frequently to work outside of it to supplement the father's income. Since home ownership and a "good job" (one in which a man used his hands and came home tired and covered with grime and perspiration) were requisites for security, that security was bought with mother's job outside the home. Police officers reminiscing about their childhood home life remember well their parents' need for security and, as we shall see, incorporated it into their own adult lives. What they do overlook in their contacts with children in neighborhoods similar to those of their childhood is that their mothers, too, were often working mothers.

Twice, so far, in the process of gathering and reporting the background data, security has been noted as a paramount factor. In the first instance, Captain Brown's annoyance at the real or implied threat to his personal adequacy reflects a psychological insecurity. The security of a job and home ownership necessary to the policeman's family in his childhood, and later in his adulthood, are on both the psychological and social levels of functioning.

The need for security was consciously stated as a major reason for joining the police force in all but two cases throughout the ranks of Eastern City's department. Security-consciousness does not end here. It is reflected in many ways throughout police work. It can be seen in the very understandable but overstated concern for an individual's protection of his own life when on duty. As often observed, police work only infrequently involves life-and-death situations. Yet, officers discuss the extremes as though they were the norm. A strong factor of social control which limits the officer from communicating dissatisfaction with assignments and departmental practices is the threat of getting a lesser position on the force and limiting the chances for promotion. This characteristic is not unique to the police but is in the forefront of concern when they are involved in daily tasks. "Should I make this arrest?" may be modified to "Should I make arrest and take the chance that someone inside or outside of the force will take offense and have me demoted or punished in some way?" Promotion is more than a reflection of achievement: it is a reaffirmation of the security mechanism.

Contrary to the findings of the study of police backgrounds, *Police Background Characteristics and Performance*, Eastern City's police backgrounds do make a difference.[3] Cohen and Chaiken report that, in their very extensive study, background was not a significant factor in predicting later performance of recruits, good or bad. The strongest predictors among New York City's police force, according to this study, was recruit training scores and probationary education.[4]

The Eastern City studies do not contradict Cohen and Chaiken on individual prediction characteristics, nor do they focus upon individual performance. What they do show, which is lost in prediction variables such as the number of commendations or citations for misconduct, is that in everyday behavior (not usually documented in the officers' folders) they consciously or subconsciously compare their own childhood socialization or upbringing with that of those with whom they come into contact.

In measuring police officers' attachment to traditional values of society, Skolnick found that over half of them considered home ownership important. He also found that

> The importance attributed to home ownership was also related to several other social characteristics. Those policemen with blue-collar fathers rate home-owning very important more often than those with white collar fathers (57 percent to 43 percent). The more regularly the policeman reported attending church, the more value he placed on home ownership.[5]

The results of the most recent study of Eastern City police agreed with those of Skolnick moreso than with Cohen and Chaiken. Like their parents, 77 percent owned their own homes; of those, 70 percent were located in or near the same area in which they grew up. Church attendance in Eastern City was erratic, and Skolnick's findings on church and home ownership were not confirmed.

Like their fathers, of whom 66 percent were blue collar workers, 59 percent of the current officers in Eastern City were blue collar workers before entering the department. Their spouses were mainly high school graduates (70 percent) and a few (7 percent) graduated from college. More than one-half of the wives were housewives. Those who were employed outside of the house were mainly engaged in some form of clerical or white collar work. They worked to supplement their husbands' incomes as did their husbands' mothers; but, as noted, the type of work was quite different.

The New York City study relegates background characteristics to a very minor position in the determination of performance. A possible explanation for the difference between the Cohen and Chaiken and the Skolnick and Eastern City studies is that New York City residents are more likely to represent "big city" attitudes than "traditional hometown" ones. New York City residents, living in a metropolitan area containing some 10 million people, are more likely to be accustomed to high-rise apartments, massive public housing projects, and large tenement buildings. They are less likely than the residents of most smaller cities throughout the United States to consider home ownership an important factor in their lives. They are less likely than their counterparts in the smaller cities and suburbs to desire car ownership. Subways and buses traverse the city of New York faster than cars plowing through streets filled with taxis, trucks, and irate pedestrians. Eastern City's police take it for granted that a car is a necessity.

What the results of the comparisons between Cohen and Chaiken and Skolnick reveal is that, compared to medium or moderate-sized communities, large cities produce as many significant differences as similarities in background characteristics.

It is a paradox that in an American society there is probably the greatest proliferation of educational facilities to be found anywhere in the world and an almost universal reluctance to accept the utility of their product, formal education.

One of the first experiences beyond familial interaction that a child in the United States becomes involved in is formal education. Compulsory as it is, the majority of individuals attends at least 12 years; and many whose familial social class standing permits or calls for college attendance continue. Some go beyond that. It would appear to be an unquestionable fact that a dominant ideological commitment is to the efficacy of formal education—and that the "American Dream" is attained through education as an institutionalized vehicle to success.

One may choose the observation of the European sociologist Stanislav Andreski: contrary to the Mertonian means-to-an-end schema—education to success—those who have amassed the greatest fortunes in America, and who in many instances lent their names and contributed large sums of money to educational foundations, were themselves unschooled.[6] A second choice with which we are perhaps more familiar is contrary to the admonition of the late warden Lewis E. Lawes of Sing-Sing Prison that "crime does not pay"—it pays well and is hardly attributable to extensive formal education.

Most people spend the better part of their childhood years in primary and secondary school because they are compelled to do so. They not only learn the formal subject matter sufficiently to move them along within the particular system, but they also learn that the diploma is the stepping stone to the next link in the institutionalized success chain. This view reaches its epitome on the college level and, for some, graduate school. The diploma is the "union card" to enter into the occupational world. It does not guarantee a job, but without it a particular job may not be attainable. From grade school through college the student receives constant feedback that what is learned in school is important but that what is learned beyond its confines is the substance of the "real world."

The "real world" is understood in concrete terms. It is known through experience. It relates to everyday life in a way one can explain through particular examples. The extraction of principles is derived from frequent observations; i.e., scientific facts, when consciously alluded to, are relatively unimportant for all practical purposes, while casual recognition of regularities in events, described as common sense, is common. Abstractions are regarded as residing in the clouds—possibly "for the birds"—and concreteness is considered down to earth! With the exception of an intellectual elite, extensive though it may be, the majority of U.S. citizens are anti-intellectual pragmatists.

The lower on the socio-economic scale people are, the more overt the anti-intellectual-pragmatic attitude they take, although practicality is not always reflected in their behavior. The police have slowly climbed the social-class ladder in their recruitment policies. Neither the watchman recruited in earlier centuries from among the aged crippled and the addle-minded nor the college-educated athlete-scholar is the norm. Depending upon whose study is cited, the police are said to be recruited from the lower socio-economic classes up to the lower-middle class. The discrepancy seems to lie more in class interpretation than in actual social backgrounds.[7] Eastern City's police are no exception. Blue collar eliminates the negative connotation of "lower" in most other designations; and, as established earlier in this chapter, blue-collar background is the mode for "the boys (and girls) in blue."

Although there is an increase in the number of police with college backgrounds or who are enrolled in college courses after their appointments, the majority of officers comes from neighborhoods near or within the ghettos and is primarily high-school educated. If anything, the increased recruitment of minority group candidates reaffirms the lower-class norm. Eastern City has had a minimum of applicants from its 1 percent black and less than 1 percent Spanish-speaking population. The average policeman in Eastern City has had at least a high school education; 85.5 percent graduated from high school and 21.1 percent had some college courses. None are college graduates. Of the three women on the force, two have had college courses and one graduated from a four-year institution. The unrealistic dream of the National Advisory Commission on Criminal Justice Standards and Goals (NACCJSG) is that

> As a condition of initial employment, candidates should have completed at least one year of education at an accredited college or university or having earned a high school diploma or its equivalent, will have met the college-education requirement within three years of initial employment. By 1982, the completion of at least four years of college education should be required as a condition of initial employment.[8]

Having established that the average citizen of the United States carries an anti-intellectual and pragmatic attitude and that the lower the social-class level the more intense the attitudes are, one recognizes that the police officer's background is not conducive to preparing for an academic experience laden with abstract principles, no matter how relevant they may be. Though he is less likely than those lower on the socio-economic scale to have dropped out of school, his commitment to schooling has generally been minimal. As noted earlier, he, as well as most members of society, has managed to earn his "union-card diploma." He may take excursions into the abstract, but he generally leaves them behind at the public school or at the police academy. As Neiderhoffer points out,

> . . . the new patrolman must resolve the dilemma of choosing between the professional ideal of police work he has learned at the Academy and the pragmatic precinct approach. In the Academy, where professionalism is accented, the orientation is toward that of the social sciences and opposed to the "Lock-them-up" philosophy. But in the precinct a patrolman is measured by his arrest record. . . . over and over again well-meaning old-timers reiterate "You gotta be tough, kid, or you'll never last."[9]

If one were to take seriously the wave of current and projected police serials on television (and probably a large portion of the viewing audience does), the overall impression would be that the police are engaged in a constant fight against crime. It would seem that the police officer's day is cluttered by extortion, rape, and murder, with an occasional robbery, and capped off with a commercial. Donald Newman writes:

> An ordinary patrol officer in a metropolitan police agency probably devotes no more than 10 to 15 percent of his time to activities directly related to law enforcement. And even here, "crime fighting" most often entails intervention in minor crime situations involving misdemeanant conduct and public order offences.[10]

Newman's description of the police officer's apportionment of time to fighting crime belies the TV public image. The Eastern City police officer is more likely to be engaged in encounters in which his weapons are quick wit and sensible talk rather than hand guns and rifles. The violence the officer sees is most often found in the urban ghetto or the poorest neighborhoods.

The promises of federal, state, and local agencies since the OEO and HUD programs of the early 1960s and the current Affirmative Action programs have done little to stem the tide of unrest in these neighborhoods. Although there are cries damning minority group members for the preferential treatment they seem to receive from some employers, their status, on the whole, is not much more improved than it was a decade ago.

The police can and do have very little effect on state and federal policies and programs. Even locally their political power as an agency is limited; thus, they can have little effect on the major problems facing their communities. Still, they are responsible for the maintenance of order in communities where disorder erupts. It would be readily conceded by all that the police are in no way equipped to deal with social problems, but until recently it has been less obvious to the general society—and most markedly unobserved by the police themselves—that they are unequipped to deal with the interpersonal problems that fill much of their time on their daily tours of duty.

It is unlikely that the political structure of the United States will change so that police, were they capable of developing solutions to attack the causes of the societal problems, will be permitted to do so. The bleak outlook is that they will continue indefinitely to focus the bulk of their attentions neither upon political intervention nor organized crime-fighting (for which they are additionally not equipped) but upon the maintenance of social order in the poor neighborhoods.

The current answer to the police officer's dilemma (presented on the following pages in the form of a focus on a specific area of interpersonal dislocations, "Family Crisis") *is in innovative educational programs.* Family-crisis-intervention training, experimented with since the beginning of the 1970s by Bard and associates, has recently spread throughout the country.[11] Presently the LEAA notes that it is funding at least six police family-crisis-intervention projects in its "Operation Demonstration" program, and some states have begun to mandate that police training include some form of programming in this area.[12]

Police departments have come a long way since the Wickersham Commission found only 20 percent of 383 cities surveyed had any formal training programs.[13] By the late 1960s the majority of cities had a variety of formal training programs of approximately 8 weeks' duration.[14] As noted earlier, the NACCJSG recommends that, in addition to the local training that state and federal (FBI) governments offer, the programs be extended and that police at all levels be encouraged, if not mandated, to take additional courses on the college level. Numerous college and graduate school programs have developed. "A report distributed by the International Association of Chiefs of Police shows that the number of community colleges offering such programs [in criminal justice] has increased from 152 in 1966-67 to 505 in 1972-73. Similarly, the number of four-year institutions offering programs has increased from 39 in 1966-67 to 211 in 1972-73."[15]

Police departments, formerly the last vestiges of the apprenticeship system of education, have succumbed, at least in theory, to the educational ideology of the United States. The means-to-the-end schema, which was reserved for many other occupational entrance and advancement areas, has spread to include police departments. Administrators want more knowledgeable officers. Officers, some ambivalent and some committed to formal education, desire exposure to more knowledge. Administrations are bolstered by such studies as that of Cohen and Chaiken, which noted that men with at least a year of college are very good officers and have fewer civilian complaints lodged against them than the average police officer. Police departments, which only a few years ago felt limited in their efficiency by restraints imposed by Supreme Court legislation, are now developing new methods of procedure through education.

Before one is carried away by such dramatic news as the development of the "thinking cop" who is destined to replace the purely "physical cop"—stereotypes at best—a good deal of what is happening in police training is reflective of that which was described earlier as the union-card-diploma approach to education. Police officers return to classroom scenes reminiscent of their prior educational experiences. They take in as much as is necessary to pass the Friday examination and wonder how much they will have to retain in order to pass the course—with precious little thought to the relevancy of the material for everyday use.

Since more police officers are assaulted while answering family-dispute calls than any other assignment, it seems to make a great deal of sense that even the departments that are somewhat reluctant to lose officers from working hours on patrol, hesitatingly, but willingly, have felt the need for "real" training.[16] Police who had sincerely (and others who had begrudgingly) been involved in training programs joined forces because they desired knowledge for its practiced implications. Eastern City police officials were among the hesitant and reluctant and took five years before they succumbed to crisis-intervention training. In short, family-crisis-intervention training is something that many police departments recognize they need rather than something that someone has merely told them that they need.

Family-crisis-intervention training programs purport to deal with crises in ways other than the traditional law-enforcement methods which either fail or aggravate the situation. The three basic aspects of these programs are: (1) the transmission of psychological and social knowledge developed in current research and theory pertaining to family stability; (2) the development of skills in interviewing, and (3) change in police attitudes about their family-crisis clients. The programs are not attempts to make "therapists" out of police officers but are aids in recognition and careful referral of family problems to appropriate agencies.

Driving an irate husband a few blocks away from home and telling him to cool off or backing him in a corner and then turning around to talk to his wife as he pounces on the officer from behind is seen by even the most anti-education individual as something less than efficient. Officers with even the slightest experience with family-dispute calls are open to potential alternatives to their own methods—if not attacked in their sensibilities. That is, if the presentation conflicts greatly with the officer's perceptions of the reality of crisis situations, he is less likely to respond favorably to the "new knowledge." The greater the involvement in the activities of the course, the greater the potential for learning. Ideally, the officer contributes to the course his experiences, the verbal reactions to subjects discussed (not lectured), the potential as an impromptu actor in a skit or as a TV cameraman taping skits, and, finally, as an analyst of the strengths and weaknesses of the approaches in the filming. Most of the subjects taught at the police academy—with the clear-cut exceptions of firearms training, self-defense, and emergency first-aid—are subjects usually presented through lectures. (It is noteworthy to mention that all three of the exceptions are most positively received by the police.) The content of the courses is discussed more than the nature of the oral presentation of the instructor. The officer is likely to talk about his own ability on the firing range, techniques of handling bleeding victims, or how he learned a particular hold or release in a self-defense class. An officer is not likely to talk about the content of a lecture on "patrol" or even how to handle a "delinquent kid." What he will discuss after the lecture is whether he enjoyed the lecturer's manner of presentation, whether the lecturer was a "nice guy" or "dull guy," a "bright one" or a "stupid one." Thousands of working hours a year are lost in unfruitful class sessions.

Family-crisis-intervention training programs range in duration, content, and manner of presentation. Courses are given, such as New York City's one-day program for all officers (with more intense courses for special units) and Eastern City's two lecture sessions, to a program of at least 40 hours of classes with follow-up programs at intervals of three, six, and twelve months. Some courses still adhere to the traditional lecture series, but most have become more involved with audiovisual aids and police participa-

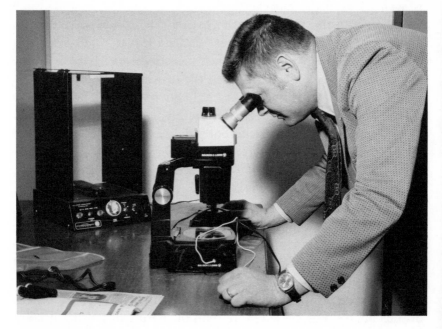

Laboratory investigation. Most medium-size police departments have minimal laboratory facilities and must depend on state police or other sources for analysis of evidence. (Bethlehem Police Dept., Bethlehem, Pa.)

tion. All deal with the criteria mentioned earlier—knowledge, skills, and attitudes. As indicated, the greater the officer participation with the program itself, the greater the program acceptance by the officers. Eastern City's lectures have been met with something less than enthusiasm by the recruits who have been exposed to the current program. One would expect them to be more enthusiastic and better trained if permitted to actively participate, rather than to merely listen to lectures. To date, no program for experienced officers has been instituted, and it is therefore impossible to predict the experienced officers' acceptance in Eastern City. One would guess that officers would respond favorably if exposed to a program with a high degree of involvement. Several experienced officers have indicated their interest in that form of training. In fact, most, if not all, of the police training (at least in the academy) could be better carried out through combinations of audiovisual presentation and role playing.

Table 1

Police Background Data

	1971 Mean Percent	1976 Mean Percent
Age		
Patrol personnel	39.0	38.3
Command personnel	47.0	46.8
Education		
Patrol		
High school diploma	85.5	81.0
Command		
Some college	21.1	53.0
Command		
High school diploma	91.0	10.0
Some college	93.0	31.0
Prior occupation		
Blue collar	59.3	35.0
White collar	29.7	21.0
Military	0.0	40.0
Other (e.g., police work, school, or no job)	11.1	4.0
Marital status		
Single	10.0	12.0
Married	88.0	77.0
Separated	0.0	6.0
Divorced	1.0	2.0
Remarried	1.0	3.0
Number of children	2.4	3.4
Home ownership		
Own	77.0	78.0
Rent	23.0	22.0
Area of residence		
North	11.0	14.0
East	11.0	16.0
Center	15.0	5.0
South	60.0	42.0
West	3.0	23.0
Father's occupation		
Blue collar	66.6	57.0
White collar	33.4	43.0
Wife's occupation		
Blue collar	9.0	12.0
White collar	29.0	15.0
Professional	3.0	14.0
Housewife	59.0	59.0

Notes

1. Sutherland, Edwin, and Cressey, Donald, *Criminology,* 9th ed. (Philadelphia: Lippincott Co., 1972); Cloward, Richard, and Ohlin, Lloyd, *Delinquency and Opportunity.*

2. Komarovsky, Mirra, *Blue Collar Marriage* (New York: Random House, 1962).

3. Cohen, Bernard, and Chaiken, Jan M., *Police Background Characteristics and Performance* (Lexington, Massachusetts: D. C. Heath and Co., 1973), p. 124.

4. Ibid.

5. Skolnick, Jerome, *Justice without Trial* (New York: John Wiley, 1967).

6. Andreski, Stanislav, "Underdevelopment and Overdevelopment," unpublished talk presented at Muhlenberg College, Allentown, Pa., March 12, 1969.

7. McNamara, John H., "Uncertainties in Police Work: The Relevance of Police Recruits Background and Training," in *The Police, Six Sociological Essays,* ed. David J. Bordua (New York: John Wiley, 1967), pp. 163-252; Niederhoffer, Arthur, *Behind the Shield: The Police in Urban Society* (Garden City, N.Y.: Doubleday & Co., 1967), pp. 37-38.

8. National Advisory Commission on Criminal Justice Standards and Goals, U.S. Department of Justice, LEAA, Washington, D.C., *Executive Summary— Reports of the NACCJS&G* 15, 1-27.

9. Niederhoffer, Arthur, *Behind the Shield,* pp. 33-34.

10. Newman, Donald J., *Introduction to Criminal Justice* (Philadelphia: J. B. Lippincott, 1975), p. 141.

11. Barocas, Harvey, "Iatrogenic and Preventive Intervention in Police Family Crisis Situations," paper presented at American Society of Criminology, Inter-American Conference, Caracas, Venezuela, November, 1972.

12. Law Enforcement Assistance Administration, "Operation Demonstration" (U.S. Department of Justice, 1975).

13. Terris, Bruce J., "The Role of the Police," in *The Annals of the American Academy of Political and Social Science,* November, 1967, p. 62.

14. Ibid.

15. Brown, Lee P., "The Police in Higher Education: The Challenge of the Times," *Criminology* 12 (May 1974), p. 121.

16. *Uniform Crime Reports,* 1973, p. 47.

Chapter **3**

FAMILY, FRIENDS, AND NEIGHBORS

IF YOU MEET a policeman* in Eastern City, he probably will be a married man, 35 years old (He is younger than his predecessor of 8 years by approximately 5 years.), the father of two children, and a home owner. Aside from the usual shop talk about such things as pay, promotions, assignments, politics, and morale, one would find him discussing kids (his own and others), the strains on his family life through the job (and not because of the persons involved), and his home and its repair. One would most likely find him talking to another policeman. Generally true of all occupationals, the assumption is that only a person in the same field of work could possibly understand the joys and agonies of the job.

All jobs are "unique" or "special" to those who are engaged in them. Police work is no different in that regard. Nevertheless, it does have its own configuration of attributes.

> There are distinctive recognizable tendencies in police as an occupational grouping. Some of these may be found in other occupations sharing similar problems. So far as exposure to danger is concerned, the policeman may be likened to a soldier. His problems as an authority bear a certain similarity to those of the school teacher, and the pressures he feels to prove himself efficient are not unlike those felt by the industrial worker. The combination of these elements, however, is unique to the policeman.[1]

---

* Policewomen will be discussed later in this chapter.

If our policeman is not engaged in discussion with a fellow officer, his talk will be either brief and cold or extended, pleasant, inconsequential patter at which he is an expert and which solidifies his relationships with his own public.

Waiting. Constant fear that one day her husband will not return home and the image provoked by thoughts of the sound of the words "killed in the line of duty" haunt police wives. Tired after a tour of duty, the officer returns home to a tense wife. Such tensions constantly produce strain on the marital life of police. (Robert Reier)

Policemen are "either-or" people. Rarely is one found who is a "middle-of-the-roader;" and if one were to ask him why, he would quickly respond that he is no wishy-washy namby-pamby. He is a real nice guy or he is a tough so-and-so! He knows that there are only good guys and bad guys in the community.[2] He is a "homebody" or he is a "police-buddy" who has plenty of time for his family or no time at all. He rarely, if ever, goes out to drink or he drinks with "the boys" frequently. He feels that he is the most important person (because of his job) in his part of town or feels totally unappreciated for all the things he does for everyone. He sees himself as the protector of society, the last bastion of patriotism and the key to the maintenance of moral order. He describes himself as a tough-and-strong and a bored-and-tired frustrated cop whose daily activity is routinely uneventful but *always* potentially dangerous. His duality continues when he discusses his family. His idealized picture is that the family is the most important part of a man's life. His wife, children, and home come before all else. His real picture includes a happy or an unhappy household marked with stresses and strain fomented by the lack of communication between husband and wife and parent and child. The lack of communication is created mostly by the unwillingness to discuss details of his work and the misunderstandings and apprehension that accompany the silence. The stresses and strains are heightened or decreased by the husband-father "homebody" or the "police-buddy" role playing, respectively.

With the exception of an occasional magazine or newspaper article and melodramatic television dramatization of *police life,* little has been written about it. It is difficult to get police officers to discuss personal matters with civilians (as all non-police personnel are called). It is even more difficult to get their permission to interview their wives and children. Permission to interview the officers is usually obtained with the proviso that the officers volunteer.[3] In turn, permission to interview wives and children rests with the officers themselves, most of whom were reluctant, during the several years of study conducted by the researcher, to grant it. Even in those cases where permission was granted, the

Hanging a closet door. There are two basic types of officers: the "police-buddies" and the "homebodies." "Police-buddies" hang around together at the local pub, complaining that shift work keeps them from their families. The "homebodies" find comfort in odd jobs around the house and consider shift work as an opportunity to be with the family more often than most people are. (Robert Reier)

family members themselves were hesitant to agree. When they did, most broke at least one appointment and some never arrived at all.

Certainly, one cannot speak quantitatively about policemen's family lives. The restrictive numbers of respondents and the voluntary nature of participation take their toll. Yet, those who did respond—policemen, wives, and children—all responded in depth with intensity of emotion and interest. Much of the story of their lives as presented in this chapter will be in the form of direct quotations. The deviation from the usual style of putting forth material is employed both to allow the reader to share directly the emotion and interest mentioned above and to allay any notions that the respondents were misrepresented. They frequently emphasized their positions on their family lives and contrasted them with examples of the family lives of other officers. (We assume these included some officers who did not volunteer to be interviewed.) The minimum age chosen for interviews with the children was 13. The youngest child to respond was 13 and the oldest 24. One officer's fiancee volunteered and was interviewed.

Frequently policemen and their families told similar tales about their lives, each often spicing their stories with "but we're different from most families." Considering the dichotomies in life-styles and the respondents' extensive overlapping details to describe them, it is most likely that a fairly accurate picture of police family life has been obtained and that any forced or non-voluntary participation attempting to achieve greater quantification would have added distortion rather than clarity and amplification of data. It should not be forgotten that the responses of the men did represent the majority of the department in numbers of responses.

> I don't associate with my neighbors. After work I'm just me. There is always somebody in the neighborhood who sees you as a policeman and most times I just want to leave the job. I have only a few friends on the police department (3 or 4) and not many friends on the outside. We (my wife and I) go out with 3 or 4 couples. Our close friends are office or steel workers. We go out to dinner, dance or visit with each other—nothing elaborate.

I suppose we have some conflict about my hunting and fishing and my job is hard on having young children [he has two]. The chances of having an argument are more [high] because of my job and on rough days when I come home, I don't want to be bothered—then we fight.

The officer speaking in the last two paragraphs can be described as a tough cop on the street, and he is generally described that way by members on the force and by others who know him. He is thought of as a nice guy off duty and he sees himself as a family man. He is a "homebody." Fixing up his home, which is rather attractive, comes after hunting and fishing; and they come after a great love and concern for his attractive wife and children. He hopes to get ahead in the department both for personal recognition and to add to his family's comfort. His wife's description of him and of their relationship differed very slightly from his own. She began:

My husband is great on hunting and fishing [as are many of the men on the force. Others frequently cite organized sports activities.] He used to be friendly with another policeman before we were married. We go out a lot by ourselves. You can't trust people anymore. They'll knife you. There are a lot of policemen who don't have all that we have [she is employed] and they are jealous. A lot don't want to be bothered with us because of that. We never left the impression that we were better than they were.

He talks little about his work and even then his answers to me are brief. I have to pump him for what I want to know. I've never noticed moods when he comes home. He's always the quiet type and he puts a lot of faith in people—more than I think he should. He's an easygoing guy.

Except for the difference in reports about friendships and a cynicism about people in general, the officer's wife's story supported his. The outstanding features of the two interviews (and other "homebody"-type interviews) are the congruence of images of the marital partners. Both are satisfied with the husband's position as a police officer and hope for, but do not expect, promotions. They emphasize the point that they do not fraternize with other officers and their families, though the husband may mention some as friends.

An ambivalence regarding the wife quoted above is noted as she describes the reason for the social distance, on the one hand the result of her mistrust of all people and on the other a form of reverse snobbery on the part of other officers and their families.

Whether they admit to much contact with other officers or to none at all, officers and their wives are sensitive about the public image of the police. Whether there is a conscious and deliberate decision not to associate with other officers' families or not, there is a feeling expressed by police and their families that they are different from the civilian public around them. It is especially true of police who do fraternize that they fit the model detailed by Gamire, Rubin, and Wilson, which states:

> The police self-image appears to be quite negative; most officers, of all ranks, seem to feel that their efforts are not well regarded or fully appreciated. Some carry this so far that they develop persecution complexes, verging on paranoia. Social contacts tend to be limited, in the main, to other police officers and their families.[3]

When they do occur, family tensions result from the husband's reluctance to discuss his work which, in turn, is attributed by his wife to his quiet nature and not to the nature of the job itself and its requirements of confidentiality. It is significant that neither he nor his wife cited changing shifts as a problem for their family life. On the contrary, when questioned about her husband's shift work, she replied, "I always tell him that he has a soft job riding around for 8 hours." She ignored the question about shifts, and when asked a second time she related some annoyance but no strong opposition to them.

Shift work plays a prominent role in the degree of satisfaction or dissatisfaction with family and work life as reported by both the "homebody" and "police-buddy" types. One sees shift work as mildly positive in that it permits him to spend more time with his wife and children than most other occupationals. The other sees shift work as negative in that it keeps him from maintaining family solidarity and creates tension. However, shift work sometimes had the reverse effect on both groups. Occasionally, an officer who may be considered a "homebody" reported that strain is created by shift work, but none of the "police-buddies" saw shift work as conducive to family life. For them, shift work always legitimized their minimal family contact or home life. It never seemed to occur to most of them that they reported spending much time with their fellow officers which could very well have been spent with their families, if they so desired. For the "homebodies" who reported dissatisfaction with shift work, their intensity was exceedingly mild. As one officer, with a smile and a mildly contemplative look, said:

> You don't get used to the hours and neither does she. It's not too bad when the kids are young but as they grow older you see problems of getting together. My wife wouldn't mind if I had weekends off, but a policeman's career is worth it. I like it. . . . Human nature is fantastic.

In further discussion he agreed that getting the older children together with their parents would be a problem in any family, with or without shifts. Meeting all types of people was compensation enough for him.

The majority of the men interviewed, both command and patrol personnel, reflected a pride in their almost unanimous response that rarely, if ever, did they discuss their work with their spouses. Implicit in their responses were two factors which contributed to their attitude. The first was a departmental policy of confidentiality about information obtained while on duty. The second was a personal, genuine concern to protect their wives and children from the knowledge of the dangers they faced—or perhaps in some instances to conceal activities that may not have been approved of at home. An assumption made by some men, and not borne out by wives' responses in general, is that wives are understanding and accepting of the code of silence. In fact, lack of communication is the most frequent cause of marital disruption in police families. The following quotations are typical of many:

> My wife is very understanding and wants me to do whatever work I want to. She doesn't like shifts and remaining home alone and I don't blame her for that. . . . I don't carry the police department home except for funny stories, no gory bits! I don't subject her to that.

Incidentally, he has been on the force for less than a year. The following two men have been on the force for about twenty years and maintained that confidentiality, combined with rotating shifts, markedly influences the splitting of their marriages. The first related:

> My wife and I don't communicate as much as we used to. By now she is accustomed to my weird hours. [This was said with a look of resignation.] She doesn't get excited about it. We don't see enough of each other. I want to nap or I leave before she's up and so on.

His interview continued with a note of dispair that his morale at home is like that at the department—bleak. (Departmental morale is discussed in chapter 7.)

The second officer was more explicit and emphatic and expressed anger in his tone:

> Since I work shifts I have no interaction with my neighbors. My salary is inadequate so I never get to give my children vacations and things other children get. There are a lot of conflicts in the family. Working as a policeman makes things difficult . . . with the children, mainly because you're not there to be the father. As they were growing up, there was a tendency to shift punishment. My wife did the punishing. The conflict between me and her [sic] has been even greater than between the kids and me. We will divorce.

The number of divorces of Eastern City police officers is not high, but talk about it is. One can speculate that the number may be as low as it is because of the officers' concern for their public image and because their idealization of the family unit holds many families together at any cost. This does not preclude the possibility that talk of divorce may be sufficient tension-release for some. More study in this area is clearly indicated. Tension in police families is frequently very high.

Divorce isn't a crime, but police wives in Eastern City are combatting it as if it were just that. The newspaper story reported by UPI, which begins with this sentence, continues to describe the situation in Seattle, Washington with the following revelation:

> When a recent survey of Seattle police indicated that almost two-thirds of the officers were divorced during the first three years of service, the police department stepped in to try to cure the marital malaise.[4]

The city of Seattle set up a ten-week course for wives to help facilitate communication and understanding between the officers and their wives. The wives were given the opportunity to vent their feelings during the course. One officer's wife reported:

> The danger is hard for a wife to take. . . . You have to be able to put it out of your mind, not to dwell on what might happen to him. If you did, you'd go nuts.[5]

Another said of the course:

> One of the early lessons especially helped. The sergeant told us that if we were going to sit around biting our nails it would drive us out of our minds. . . . He said we have to be casual about things other wives aren't.

Still another took a fatalistic view:

> Every day he leaves the house I know he has a chance of never returning. I have to understand this and then take the fatalist's view and go on about my daily life normally.[6]

Writing about the Denver police in 1962, Mort Stern claimed that:

> As a group, policemen have a very high rate of ulcers, heart attacks, suicides, and divorces. These things torment him too [in addition to tensions and fears on the job]. Divorce is a big problem for policemen. A man can't be a cop for eight hours and then just turn it off and go home and be a loving father and husband—particularly if he's just had somebody die in the back of his police car.[7]

Rotating shifts, fear of potential dangers, and secrecy take their toll on the nerve centers of police family life. Stern continued:

> Part of the tensions [he carries home from the job] come from the incredible monotony. He is cooped up with another man, day after day, hour after hour, doing routine things over and over. The boredom of routine makes him want to scream sometimes. The excitement that most people think of as the constant occupation of policemen is so infrequent as to come as a relief.[8]

Part of the tension comes as a side effect of the secrecy factor. Suspicion is contagious. Policemen are notoriously suspicious of everybody, including their families. The fiancee of a policeman explained that she, at first, was furious about the idea that her intended husband followed her whether he was on or off duty. She resented his distrust. As time went on, she reported, she became accustomed to his surveillance. She accepted the idea that a police officer simply has to be suspicious, and she turned a negative situation into a positive one by concluding that she even found it cute that he was so jealous of her.

The contagion of suspicion was reflected in the earlier report of the wife who said "you can't trust anyone," and a few wives explicitly extended this point of view to include their husbands. Wives suspect their husbands of cheating on them—and not without reason. In the following report by a young police officer, who is otherwise happily married, he expresses a tension created by his wife's distrust and the circumstances that could place him in an awkward situation. He summed up his marital story as follows:

> When I told my wife I was going to be a policeman she wasn't overjoyed, but she doesn't interfere with what I want to do. She was concerned that I get enough pay to live with. At first she worried about me getting shot at but she knows that I'm in charge. She is proud and if she's still scared, she's hidden it. I tell her not to worry, but I'm sure she does inwardly. . . . The only problem in my family is with my wife thinking that you run around, but it's a lot of bull! We get involved with people of no morals and it takes a superman to turn down sex and all that!

Everyone feels that his problems are greater than everyone elses'. As a group police believe they are the most misunderstood people. Each individual knows that he is the least comprehended. Stern says:

> The cop begins to think of himself as a member of the smallest minority group in the community. The idea gradually sinks in that the only people that understand him, that he can be close to, are his fellow officers. His associations become even further limited and he begins to believe the old phrase, "Nobody likes us, so to hell with them."[9]

Both "homebodies" and "police-buddies" report that they have friends on and off the department rolls. "Homebodies" occasionally emphasize that they do not usually associate with fellow officers. Some, in extended conversations, do admit to a fairly close association with men on their shifts. As one man aptly put it, "You usually find most of your friends from your job. Where I was before, I was with them. Policemen go with policemen. They share interests." Curiously enough, he shares golfing with fellow officers, a sport that he could enjoy with members of any other occupation as well. As Skolnick and others have pointed out, although other occupationals have a consciousness of kind, none are as close-knit, nor do they show such a uniformly consistent view of the world, as a police officer. A good description of police camaraderie was given by one man who noted, "Within police departments, there are cliques within cliques and it's basically true that policemen hang around with policemen."

One man who forcefully claimed that he did not associate with other officers while off duty gave a lengthy report of why he did not. He stated that he neither smoked nor drank alcoholic beverages and that a lot of the men do. Although he insisted that he was not against drinking, he spoke with disdain about the drinking groups that form and the loose behavior of those men and the wives who join in with them. An officer's wife who described her life as a happy one felt that she and her husband maintained a good relationship with the others on the force by keeping a social distance and only infrequently attending police functions, such as picnics. She described herself as older, from another generation, one which did not include "having to get married" and filled only with thoughts of sex. The new generation, she summed up, is "vulgar and young."

Perhaps the most extreme example of the "police-buddy" type was reported by a wife whose adjustment to life seemed to reflect that a marriage, a home, and security is all that she should want or expect. She could not conceive of life's being any different from what it was. In a matter-of-fact way she said, "He [her husband] grew up with hoods and later he went with his friends into the bar. He still has some of his old bar friends but now he has golfing friends and policemen too." His policemen friends were divided into those who shared one or both of his favorite activities. He, in turn, suggested that she find friends of her own. She actually attempted to do so but found that single women appeared to have nothing in common with her and married women were usually in the company of their husbands. Between her husband's shift work, her own employment, and his socializing with "the boys," her activities are summed up by her statement, "I am so alone." Their marriage survives because of her minimal expectancies and her respect and admiration for her husband because of his occupation.

Husbands are not as considerate of wives when commenting about barroom excursions, as evidenced by the statement of the husband of the woman above. When he responded to questions about shift work and about his off-duty activities, he gave the same retort both times: "She's got to put up with it!"

Both wives and children of policemen, for the most part, reflect a pride in the policeman in their family. "Homebody" policemen find time to be with their wives and children. According to the responses of their families, those officers spend more time than the average worker can spend with his family. Whether this is actually the case is not as important as the perception of it. Spending time with the family in the home and in the community is the norm for them. It is not unusual for these families to have another police-man among their relatives. Often, the husband or wife was the son or daughter, nephew or niece of a police officer. In any case, contacts with other relatives on a frequent basis is reported more often by "homebodies" than by "police-buddies." When not engaged in social activities, the "homebody" rates house repair high.

Most, if not all, police join and remain in the Fraternal Order of the Police. Some join fraternal groups such as the Masons, Moose, or local fire company's social program. Interestingly enough, although there is no consistent pattern in Eastern City, men who say they go to church often are mainly from the "homebody" group. Both groups find that they cannot attend any activity with 100-percent regularity because of their shift work. The exceptions are among the command or officers with regular day assignments.

Children of policemen report that it is embarrassing while in grade school to have a father who is a policeman. Both boys and girls report that they eventually lose their feeling of embarrassment and gain a feeling of pride. Some use their relationship to get privileged positions in their cliques. Daughters of officers say that boys are more careful about how they behave and treat them with greater respect than that which is generally shown other girls. Officers' sons, on the other hand, did not gain greater respect from any of their peers but did agree with the girls who said that their friends always expected them to be "good," or at least to behave somewhat better than the rest of the crowd. Girls seemed to use their special status more than boys. One woman, who spoke very favorably about her present relationship with her father, said that although her father did not understand her when she was younger, she always felt safe and secure, ". . . because he was often at home when I got there and later when I worked at night, he would follow me home in a police car or I'd call the police to escort me home at midnight." In retrospect, she volunteered, "Something I thought about lately is that everybody knows what Daddy makes and people place you in a particular class, but we were better off than most. Incidentally, Mother worked and I thought our life was kind of nice."

The children interviewed unanimously indicated that their fathers were strict. Some felt the restrictions which were imposed upon them by their fathers were too severe, while others did not.

Generally, they felt that their fathers were right to be strict since their fathers knew (and told them about) "bad kids" and what happened to them. A few of the boys said that the treatment was not only right, but also fairly administered. Girls did not consider the question of fairness at all. Their evaluations were measured in right or wrong and not in fair or unfair.

Children did not express the fear of danger for their fathers that their parents conveyed. Their faith and pride in their fathers obliterated any such ideas. A typical answer to a question concerning a child's perception that the mother was perhaps fearful was, "No, I don't think he is in real danger. I never think about it anyway." The respondent, a young woman, did not consider that her mother might harbor feelings different from her own. Boys were more likely to answer that their mothers were fearful but that they were not.

Children shared the view of their fathers that the entire family is always in public view. As mentioned earlier, their friends reinforce this view when they expect them to be model children. According to the children, others with whom they came in contact held similar expectations. Some of the children attempted to prove their normalcy to friends by behavior short of juvenile delinquency (or so they stated). Others said they tried to live up to the model. In summary, the respondent children were from "homebody" families and clearly expressed a minimum of tensions within their families. They displayed a fair amount of tension in trying to maintain a wholesome public image while growing up. Unfortunately, it is impossible to do little more than speculate about the possible responses of children of "police-buddy" families. The voluntary nature of participation and the dependency of approval by parents for children's participation left little chance that they would respond. Future research designs may overcome this weakness and hopefully will shed some light on the similarity and/or differences between children of both types of police families.

Policewomen in Eastern City are too few in number to imply that they are representative of policewomen in cities of similar size. If one looks at the Uniform Crime Reports of the F.B.I., a scan of their police statistics reveals that cities the size of Eastern City employ from 0-3 policewomen. Eastern City employs three. Two women serve on patrol duty, a job usually reserved for men, and one serves in the traditional position of juvenile officer. Neighboring cities have yet to add *patrolwomen* to their police forces, although they do have *policewomen.*

Women have been in police work in America since the middle of the nineteenth century. It was assumed then, and still is believed by many police administrators and their staffs, that women could serve in the functions of matron or counsellor to women and young children but were not physically or mentally capable of coping with the duties involved in police patrol work.

A recent book has aptly noted the changing status of women in police work:

> The worth of the female in the police service has been greatly underestimated. Female police officers are as much a minority as blacks, Orientals, Mexicans, and other ethnic groups. However, the police are venturing from traditional bounds and meeting contemporary issues with innovative techniques. For example, Pennsylvania State Police, The Texas Department of Public Safety, The New York City Police, to name but a few, now have women officers. The women of the Pennsylvania State Police perform normal patrol duties and are assigned to both one and two-officer patrol units. Domestic disturbance teams, police intervention units, police-court liason offices are using women and minorities to a greater degree.[11]

Interviewing Eastern City's policewomen is doubly rewarding for the male researcher. The women are extremely articulate and exceptionally attractive. The occasional glimpses of policewomen on national television or in newspaper reports could lead one to speculate about beauty as a prerequisite for appointment. Eastern City's policewomen and their executives in the department cite the superior scores of the women on Civil Service examinations as sufficient evidence that the jobs were achieved by merit alone. The oral and physical exams are secondary to the written exam, one is assured.

Crunch. Policewomen are as likely to be found making out accident reports, directing traffic, or grappling with a mugger as they are in the traditional job of working with women and children, but their full acceptance by both the public and the force is far off. (Call-Chronical Newspapers, Allentown, Pa.)

The superior scores on written examinations reflect one of the marked differences between the policewomen and the policemen. The educational level of the three women averages out to two years of college, and for the men the average is a little more than two years less. A second exception, casually noted above, is that the women are very articulate. The major exceptions end with the motivational difference for entering police work. The women expressed for themselves, and in their expectancies for other women who would join the department, that the *excitement* of policework, and not its security, is paramount. Their preparation in college was specifically designed to meet a vocational interest in policework or a related field.

Excitement, variety, liking people, and a chance to "make good money" is a composite of the reasons Eastern City's policewomen joined the department. Earning a salary equal to that which men in the same job receive, rather than the security of the income, was the way the women interpreted their comments about "good money." None had relatives on the force nor did they have any prior contact with police work before their current employment.

Eastern City's policewomen were not all lifelong residents, but they all indicated they had been raised in basically similar neighborhoods with backgrounds similar to the men.[12] They were less guarded about their comments, and although they told the interviewer that they were specifically commanded by a senior officer not to reveal departmental secrets or views, they were not the least bit hesitant to discuss the department or, for that matter, anything about themselves. One laughingly said, "I frankly don't know what it is that I'm not supposed to talk about. I don't know any department secrets!"

An example of the frankness of the policewomen was revealed in an anecdote in which Mary* revealed her hostility to blacks and to other women. She detailed the story of several encounters with women, both black and white. Mary said that she counteracted her hostility with an exceptionally courteous manner on numerous

---

* A fictitious name, as are all others in reporting these interviews.

occasions. The responses she received, she said, were more often clouded by disdain than by respect. Then one day she lost her temper and bullied a black girl. She found an immediate rapport with the girl. At that point in the interview Mary seemed to genuinely discover that perhaps in her earlier encounters she appeared phony and unreal.

Jane found that women resent being stopped or arrested by her. She, Mary, and Ruth agree that women, when arrested, often attempt to use their feminity on male officers with some success. They cannot do this with patrolwomen. Male officers, they said, have a tendency to expect them to make the arrests whenever women are involved. This is a carryover from the earlier days when women in police work worked only with other women and/or children. All of Eastern City's policewomen were at one time attached to the Juvenile Bureau where that philosophy still applies, but to a lesser degree.

Patrolwomen resented the attitude of male officers who make such distinctions as "male" or "female" arrests made respectively by male or female officers. Nevertheless, female officers do feel freer to physically restrain women, while the men hesitate to do so. When women officers arrest men they do not feel as restricted about using physical force as male officers do with women. In fact, in order to prove their equality to the male officers, to be "just one of the *guys,*" in the presence of one or more male officers for backup assistance they have welcomed the opportunity to show that they can subdue men as well as women.

There was some selectivity in the female officers' choice of candidates for combat. None of Eastern City's patrol officers nor its policewomen are hefty; therefore, either young men in their late teens who are slim in stature or frail older men are prime targets. Actually, women are more likely to charm the offender into submission than to bruise him. As Mary said, several men have told her, "I'm glad you arrested me rather than a man." This implies that female officers are not as likely as the men to treat prisoners roughly.

Off-duty shock. Policewomen are not different from policemen or civilians. They receive department-store bills too. They do differ from patrolmen, however, in that they are better educated and more attractive. (Robert Reier)

Male traffic offenders are doubly irritated when stopped by policewomen. Women offenders are known to occasionally use their wiles to get a policeman to give them another chance. Men, Jane said, "turn on the charm" but to no avail. When they recognize that their charm has not achieved the desired effect, they are not only annoyed at receiving a ticket but they are additionally crushed and their egos are shaken. Women traffic violators, like other women offenders, are frequently arrogant to female officers. Some are annoyed at the lack of opportunity to smile coyly at a traffic cop.

In recent years, Eastern City's policewomen have been the subject of interviews by TV stations and the local press. They are accustomed to questions about their relationships in the department and in the community. With the advent of the patrolwoman and the assumption of an equality of status with men on the force, it is not uncommon for them to respond to questions specifically related to the acceptance men show to them within the department. They seem to thoroughly enjoy their "celebrity" status, while at the same time they yearn to be "just one of the *guys*." They delight in recounting stories about "holding their own" in making an arrest in the presence of policemen. At the next moment, they revel in the fact that most of the men in the department and a great many on the street recognize their beauty with whistles, catcalls, and enticing remarks. Most of the remarks, they explain, are of the harmless, flirtatious variety and are enjoyed for the moment and then ignored.

If male officers, especially some of the older men, appear to be protective of their female counterparts—and Mary, Jane, and Ruth say they are—then it is appropriate to note that the women "mother-hen" the men. The policewomen are very conscious of the concern that the policemen's wives have about their spouses working with women day and night. They are, according to their statements, inordinately careful to attend social events where they can assure wives that they are not intimately involved with their husbands. They do enjoy the company of police officers off duty and do not hesitate to say so.

The "mother hen" comes out in each of the policewomen as they individually described the dilemmas of policemen. They have observed that policemen have greater opportunity for indiscretion than "civilians" do and that the problems are compounded by the fact that there are "many women who cannot resist a uniform." As Ruth stated, "Even the ugliest dog in the department looks good to them."

Insufficient pay, easy access, stolen property, offers of bribes, a youth spent on the borderline between honesty and dishonesty, and a compulsion to prove masculinity—all exert pressure on the policeman to lose control. The "mother hens" take every opportunity to remind the men of their responsibilities. They are also quick to praise and defend the men. They aver that the majority of the men do not succumb to temptation. Their words are full of emotion as they reflect on those men who do stray. They feel sadness, sympathy, and anger. Along with the mothering, one might say they are also "brothering" (not sistering) as they commiserate with the rest of the force over the shame that is cast upon them all.

In citing citizen and department impressions of them, the women divided both groups by age, and the citizens were again divided by sex. Citizens generally seemed surprised that there were women patrol officers. Younger people were usually very accepting of them although some would snicker or make "wisecracks." Older people were either skeptical or disapproving, but not the very old, who were more like the young in their attitudes. The difference between the responses of the civilians and the policemen in each age group was the intensity of the latter. They had more reason to be serious about their answers.

The "die-hard" old-time officer often based his hostility to women officers on the oft-heard argument that women are not physically capable of defending themselves in a brawl or in backing up a male partner in combat. Some old-timers saw women as a novelty and a nuisance, as well. Younger men usually welcomed them although they, too, sometimes were doubtful about the back-up help—or they simply felt that women should be found at home as housewives.

In chapter 2 it has been established that women working outside the household are not uncommon in the lives of policemen. What men actually resent is women in occupations which help to reinforce masculinity, such as police work. What will policemen use as a yardstick for measuring their masculinity if women prove capable of performing police tasks?

A final word or two about Mary, Jane, and Ruth. They enjoy policework at least as much or more than the men in their platoons and department. This may be so partly because of their preferred status, though they would vehemently deny it, and partly because their occupational choice was made because of the work itself and not for the security the position offered.

Two of the three women expressed themselves strongly in accord with much of the current women's liberation philosophy. One is single, one is separated, and one is remarried. In discussing marriage, they cast off the liberated position and described a future committed to traditionalism, primarily because they believe this would be desired by their spouses.

Lastly, they enjoy the support of civilian women who admire them for their liberated occupations, and they understand fully the scorn of those women who see them as too liberal. They, too, idealize the image of wife and mother at home, although their current behavior contradicts that image.

Notes

1. Skolnick, Jerome, "Why Police Behave the Way They Do," in *Police in America,* ed. Jerome Skolnick and Thomas Gray (Boston: Educational Associates, 1975), p. 31.

2. See Chapter 4.

3. Gamire, Bernard I., Rubin, Jesse, and Wilson, James Q., *The Police and the Community* (Baltimore: Johns Hopkins Univ. Press, 1972), p. ix.

4. Sweet, Robert E., "Seattle Police Wives Learning about Husbands' Jobs," *Allentown* (Pa.) *Sunday CALL-Chronicle,* June 13, 1971, p. C-15.

5. Ibid.

6. Ibid.

7. Stern, Mort [and a former Denver police officer], "What Makes a Policeman Go Wrong?" in *The Ambivalent Force,* ed. Arthur Niederhoffer and Abraham Blumberg (Waltham, Mass.: Ginn and Company, 1970), p. 127.

8. Ibid.

9. Ibid.

10. Skolnick, "Why Police Behave the Way They Do," p. 343.

11. Waldron, Ronald J., Uppa, Jagdish C., Quarles, Chester L., McCauley, R. Paul, Harper, Hilary, Frazier, Robert L., Benson, James C., and Altemose, John R., *The Criminal Justice System: An Introduction* (Boston: Houghton Mifflin Co., 1976), p. 116.

12. See Chapter 2.

Chapter **4**

WHOM DO YOU TRUST?

"Why are you looking at me that way?"

"What way?"

"You know what way."

How often have we heard the above conversation or participated in a similar one ourselves? We take it for granted that when we know someone well, we know what he thinks; and we become doubly irritated when he answers us with a confused or defensive reply. The certainty of our assumption magnifies our irritation; our irritation triggers our ensuing behavior. The objects of our anger can attempt to deny, move away from us, or agree. If they agree, their own anger may be internalized for the sake of harmony; or, in some instances, they may agree because they see and believe what we seemed to see in them. Obviously, in these situations there are more chances for misunderstanding than chances for understanding.[1]

Robert Bierstedt, in *The Social Order,* has said that where the differences among people are great, conflict is slight. Where the differences are slight, people tend to magnify them, and conflict is great.[2] We could add that many times we may *magnify* the conflict situations when we *assume* the differences to be slight.

Frequently, there are significant differences in the backgrounds of seemingly similar people that create "glass walls," or invisible barriers to mutual understanding.

Claiming a working-class background, as the police most often do—that is, being raised in the ghetto or on the fringe of it and

56

participating in similar childhood experiences in the streets, schools, or churches—does not eliminate ethnic, national-heritage, racial, or familial differences and all the many nuances within their configurations. It was no problem during childhood and especially in adolescence to be actively aware of the differences between

Lost. Whether a crying child is black or white, the policeman's heart is with her as he prepares to locate her home and take her there. He assumes he knows minority people well, since he has resided in the same neighborhood, but he may overlook the different cultural backgrounds involved. (Robert Reier)

oneself and the neighbor kids and to define them with derogatory names such as "Kike," "Wop," "Squarehead," or "Mick." For those who remain socially and culturally within the boundaries of their original heritage and for those whose adult life-patterns expand into society's ways, their perceptions of each other's ideas and the meaning of each other's behavior becomes distorted.

It is less of a social problem for people who claim to be or who are separated by social-class distance to distort their perceptions of each other than for those who claim to share social-class similarities, since in the second instance actual contact and potential for conflict are greater than in the first. Such persons are prone to make many more assumptions about each other than do those who are socially distant. It is of little consequence if a working-class man thinks that millionaires spend all their time loafing around on beaches around the world. His misconception will not create any hardships for himself or the millionaires. He is not likely to interact with millionaires, and the amount of time that he thinks about them at all will be relatively brief. On the other hand, he may entertain thoughts about other working-class people. If, for example, he is working and they are not, he probably will express hostility toward them. Unemployed working-class people are not people who live in big mansions far away; they are "lazy bums who live down by the bank of the creek," whom he has seen boozing away the few dollars they have "chiseled from the welfare department." The police are guilty of wider misconceptions than those generally held in society. This leads to misunderstanding, hurt, and suspicion.

Jerome Skolnick, in *Justice without Trial,* pointed out that although in principle the police of Eastville and Westville (pseudonyms of two communities he studied) were, like most police in the United States, not racially biased, in practice the blacks of those towns regarded them as highly biased.[3] With few exceptions, both patrolmen and "brass" in one of the Eastern City studies reflected the theme expressed in Westville and Eastville: "We treat everybody alike."[4] The police officer resents any implication that different or preferential treatment would be given because of race, social class, or any other reason. In fact, it is significant that he initially rejects any form of social-class categorization of people in his community. Nevertheless, for whites, he creates his own classifications, such as "poor people," "bums," "welfare chiselers," "big-shot rich people," and "those like me." For blacks, he substitutes "the older families, good people who have lived here a long time," "migrant trash," and "those like me." His major segregation is between the "good people" and the "bad ones"—that is, those who like and respect the police and those who dislike and are disrespectful to the police.

The policeman is usually unaware of the inconsistencies in his attitudes. Although he rejects general social-class and racial categorization, he creates his own highly subjective and prejudiced stereotypes. When the policeman claims "We treat everybody alike," he has incorporated into his ideas about people one or another relatively superficial similarity that he shares with members of each social-class level, white or black. Once he has done so, he can simply divide his fellow men into "good guys" and "bad guys." For lower-class people he generalizes similarity in the area of place of residence: "I was brought up in the same section of town." For the middle class he refers to occupation: "They have to work hard, just like me." For the upper class he must reach out with "They're people too." Although the policeman believes that he has now equalized all people to a single level and therefore deals with them equally as either "good guys" or "bad guys," this level of reasoning is superficial, and his predisposition toward interaction with them is not based on it. As Sagarin says, to say two things are similar is not to imply that they are identical or even that they are alike in any other way than in their particular points of similarity.[5]

The policeman in Eastern City, after comfortably establishing his own social-class divisions, categories that use descriptive labels rather than technical language (which he rejects), proceeds during his interview to eliminate the wealthy black as nonexistent and thus not relevant for discussion.* As he says, in confirmation of the Bierstedt principle of social distance, "If there are any [wealthy blacks], they don't bother me."

---

* There are no wealthy blacks in Eastern City and only a few prosperous, management-level blacks.

The blacks constitute a little more than 1 percent of the population of this medium-sized city and with few exceptions reside in a single geographical area. When he gets intensely involved in his discussion of the blacks, the patrolman makes few distinctions on the basis of class symbols such as more expensive homes and better occupations among blacks. Whether they keep the homes clean and neat, home ownership, and steady employment are more important to him. After all, he assumes, neat homes, home ownership, and steady employment all indicate responsible, nice people who will create few problems for him. He sees only a single neighborhood for blacks. As he uses the term "blacks" only sparingly and in public, it is more accurate to say that he sees only "niggers" or "jigs."

Bayley and Mendelsohn say that "Negroes do not enter into nor walk away from contact with the police indifferently. On the contrary, it is terribly significant for them, and they learn from it. It does affect their perceptual world."[6] The police do not enter into contact with the black indifferently either. Policemen are highly suspicious of all people. This is a built-in characteristic of their profession. They are especially suspicious of blacks. Why?

Earlier we noted that where differences are slight, there is a tendency to magnify them and create conflict. The policeman came out of the same neighborhood, went to the same school, and probably fought in the same school yard as the black. His family was just as poor as the black's is now, especially if he was a child during the Great Depression years. In these respects the differences between them are slight; they share a "poor kid" background. According to Sagarin, although in the dominant characteristics they are alike, their differences will be elaborated and exaggerated; racial, cultural, and religious differences will loom large. The policeman is a member of the white majority (consisting of minorities of the past—and present), and the blacks are a minority group. The policeman conveniently overlooks the fact that he is quite often from the dominant national stock in his city and was raised with a particular cultural heritage (German in this instance).

He sees himself simply as "American." The blacks, with their "soul food" and other cultural traits, seem very different from him. Soul food is different. African clothes, hair styles, and names are different, as is black music. Police know it, and blacks affirm the differences with the resounding cry "Black is beautiful!"

The policeman considers himself an astute judge of people. He knows that his job calls for quick analysis of troublesome situations and people, and he sizes up social types (or stereotypes) routinely. Since he frequently shares the dominant characteristic of "poor kid" background, he assumes he understands the black. As he observes the differences between himself and the blacks in that "same" environment, he assumes that he understands the reasons for those differences. But he does not. The ways and the meanings of blackness and black behavior are foreign to the white policeman. When blacks then act in ways the policeman does not understand, he is more disconcerted than if he had not thought he understood them. He becomes more suspicious of blacks than of whites.

It is important to note that the policeman's prejudices may not be significantly different from those of most white Americans. He may even know, as other whites do, many of the standard explanations given for the depressed lot of the black American in the United States and may be sympathetic or hostile. What places him in a unique position is that he is in an occupation that calls for contact with blacks more often than most other jobs whites are in, and that he meets blacks more frequently in stressful circumstances. The most critical point is that with heightened suspicion and negative expectations, his predisposition is to act in a hostile manner toward blacks and treat them with less genuine consideration than he would whites.

Picture a Cadillac with a dented front fender nestled snugly around a telephone pole, one wheel on the sidewalk and the other hanging over the gutter. The policeman who sees this sight approaches rapidly. He sees the occupant, a white man dressed in a new suit, sitting forlorn. The wheels click swiftly and automatically for the officer. Here is a businessman who went a little too fast around the corner and up on the curb. He is either a decent, fairly wealthy guy or a "big shot"; that is, he is either a good guy who rates respect or a "wheel" who demands respect and who could make it tough it he doesn't get it. Thinking time is over, and the patrolman asks the car's occupant in a concerned tone, "What happened, sir?"

Let us take the same scene and replace the white driver with a black one. The same concerned policeman approaches rapidly. He sees the occupant, a black man dressed in a new suit, sitting forlorn. The wheels click swiftly and automatically for the officer. Here is a black "dude" tearing up the streets with a big Cadillac, which is probably going to be repossessed by the finance company—if anything is left of it by the time this jerk gets finished with it. Thinking time is over, and the patrolman says to the car's occupant in a flip tone, "Get out fella. Where the hell did ya think ya were going?"

It is probable that, in either example, the policeman's very first question on seeing the occupant would have been whether he was injured. Had either man been injured, the policeman would have tended to him with concern regardless of color. But if there was no injury, the officer would have shown no genuine consideration for either man.

Two white boys, about 15 years of age, are punching each other while standing on the corner of an upper-middle-class neighborhood. A police car approaches. The boys stop fighting, and as the officer leaves his car the boys watch and decide between themselves who is going to "rap" with the "cop." The officer warns the boys and tells them to move along. If they are "too disrespectful," he takes them home, and their parents are cautioned either by the officer or later on by a juvenile-bureau officer.

Two black boys, about 15 years of age, are punching each other while standing on a corner in one of the poorest neighborhoods in town. A police car approaches. The boys stop fighting and "split" in opposite directions. Depending on how long it takes the officer to catch the boy he decides to chase (if he does catch him at all) and the difficulties encountered in making the chase, the officer may deal summarily with him. He may decide to "run the kid in to the station and book him." His decision to do so could stem from his sustained anger, developed and heightened by the chase; from a preconceived idea that the black boy comes from a broken home and needs the discipline that the police, courts, and other authorities can give him; or, in fewer instances, from a genuine concern to provide the boy with greater guidance.[7]

The policeman's prejudgements decidedly play a significant part in the way that he responds. Nevertheless, it should not be overlooked that he follows up that initial response with a second one, which depends more on the behavior of the assumed offender than on preconceived notions. If the white driver expresses hostility, the officer will probably match him word for word. If the black driver acts courteous and humble, his remaining contact may even be described as pleasant. Similarly, if the two white boys run away, or if the two blacks remain to talk with the officer, the white rather than the black boys would probably be detained.

It is clear that the policeman's prejudices cue his initial responses to members of various groups, but it cannot be overlooked that his subsequent action is influenced by observed behavior. The deference of the person to the authority of the officer, as long as the officer assumes that it is genuine, overrides or at least subdues further responses.

Police officers whose assignments bring them into frequent contacts with minority people form intense attitudes toward them, pro or con, but even a pro attitude is basically less positive than the officers' favorable attitude toward members of the white majority. It would seem that greater contact is not the key to decreasing suspicion.[8] An officer expressing a "pro" position reported that "most of them [blacks] are pretty good people. I never had no [sic] trouble with them. They toe the line in your presence, but they stick together." For this officer, although he expresses a positive position, his suspicion of blacks as a group is reflected in the key phrases "in your presence" and "but they stick together." Another patrolman assigned to the same area complained bitterly that "those wise militants demand their rights and openly challenge you." Still another sneered, "I have no use for them." Then he added, "But then, I have no use for lazy whites either." Once he had established equal treatment as his stated position as indicated in his comment about whites, he went into a tirade about a black who had "beat up his own crippled mother and stole her welfare checks." From that point on there was no attempt on his part to cover up his contempt for and distrust of blacks.

Most of Eastern City's police "brass" reported favorable opinions of blacks. Frequently, they would comment that the majority of blacks have respect for law and order and think that the local police are "O.K." Because of their positions in the department, they rarely come in contact with blacks. As was true of some patrolmen, the "brass" spoke quite favorably about the older black residents. "It is the younger black or the migrant that agitates," or, "Thank God that the older people keep us 'posted' [informed]," they would say. One command officer spoke with great praise the blacks' [good sense in the] treatment of him when he was called to quell a potential riot of about 100 blacks assembled in the streets.

Beyond the glowing statements about cooperation of the blacks, there were generalized comments such as "I read, if over 5 percent of the blacks are troublemakers, you have a good chance of a riot." "I pity them [blacks]." "They have a deep-rooted animosity for us."

The "brass" are also more likely than the patrolmen to talk at length about their resentment of legislation that they feel favors blacks over patrolmen. They do not usually interact with blacks and do not hold as intense feelings as the officer on the street. Still, a former police officer, now holding an elected county law-enforcement position, who was interviewed more than two years earlier, asked the author at a chance meeting, "Are you still interviewing cops to get them to love blacks?"

One way to summarize the relationship of the police to minorities other than blacks is to note that as "blackness" and "black ways" are foreign to the white policeman, so too are the Spanish language of Puerto Ricans and other Latins, and the ideas, ideals, and appearance of both youths and morals offenders. Although these groups are foreign to the policeman, he assumes that he understands them. As with blacks, when they do not conform to his expectations, he resents them and is suspicious of them. Only greater awareness of the differences and the meaning of those differences for minority peoples will decrease the police officer's hostility, suspicion, and predisposition to act negatively toward them.

Ex-convicts are an example of the nonracial, nonethnic group that Sagarin calls "the other minorities" and are a group that policemen encounter frequently. One would expect police suspicion toward this group to be high, and it is. In addition, the police officer has as little awareness of ex-cons' attitudes toward him as of other minority groups' attitudes. He sees the ex-con as simply a "bad guy," but the ex-con has a less simplistic attitude about policemen.

Much has been written about the usual minorities' attitudes toward policemen, but little has been written about the ex-cons' attitudes. Therefore, to test the notion that the policeman fails to comprehend the attitudes of "the other minorities" as well as those of blacks, a study of the attitudes of ex-cons was carried out by the author in 1969.[9] The description of that study on the following pages confirms the notion and provides the kind of information that the police should have when dealing with that minority.

James Wilson has noted that the police officer's common categorization of people as simply "good guys" or "bad guys" is oversimplified. There are many factors that confound society's image of the policeman. He has asked, "To what extent do police officers perceive citizens as hostile?"[10] The people the police see as "good guys" are not necessarily supporters of the police and their practices.

If the police are wrong about the general population's view of the police as a group, is it possible that their perception of the position of the law violator or "bad guy" is equally incorrect? Undoubtedly their perception of the public's attitude toward them not only affects their morale but also largely determines their behavior toward each segment of the population with which they come into contact. Is the law-violator's image of the police congruent with the image police believe ex-convicts have of them? Since, as noted earlier, the good guys in the society do not necessarily like the "men in blue," could it be that the bad guys in the society do not simply dislike the police?

The research on the ex-convict was carried out in the same area where the Eastern City police department is the largest of several forces. As could be expected, many of the ex-convicts in the study alluded directly to the Eastern City force.

The ex-convicts were not as easily located as police—that is, easily located under the primary criterion that they be involved in the study of their own volition and not by official direction. The police who responded to the questionnaires in the earlier part of the study knew the researcher and were volunteers. Their positions on the force were not likely to be affected by their responses and they knew it. The responses of the ex-convicts, on the other hand, could not be assured to be free of bias if the respondents were referred to the researcher by an official agency such as a parole department. The lack of a long-standing informal relationship between the researcher and the ex-convicts and the lack of assurance that the material gathered would not be used by the parole department made the use of direct referral from that department unsuitable. In the cases of both police and ex-convicts, although a more complete, representative sample would have been desirable, the research assumption that a more truthful answer would be obtained from volunteers overrode any idea of compelling them to respond by official command. A plan was designed to reach ex-convicts unofficially.

In Eastern City there was an ex-convict we shall call Earl who had maintained himself satisfactorily in the community for about a dozen years after a period of approximately 30 years of incarceration in various prisons. He opened up his home as a temporary shelter for other ex-convicts. In order to get support to establish a permanent Halfway House in his home, Earl made himself known in civic circles and wherever people permitted him to speak of his project. The researcher made it known to Earl that he would like to speak to him and others about their attitudes toward the police. In the summer of 1969 the word was spread. In the fall, mainly through repeated contact with the Halfway House director, respondents slowly dribbled in to be interviewed.

While the study was under way, a group of ex-convicts, members of the *Fortune Society,* a group whose purpose is to disseminate information about prison conditions, sent representatives into the area for a speaking engagement, and they too were questioned. They could be considered either representative of a subgroup of ex-convicts who are highly articulate or not representative because they were articulate and eager to respond. They did, in either case, meet the qualification of responding voluntarily.

The study did not separate responses of traditional minority groups from those of others but recognized "that abusive treatment of minority groups [by the police] and the poor continues to occur," giving rise to the likelihood that responses of ex-convicts who were from minority groups may have been dominated by minority-group rather than ex-convict reactions.[11]

The majority of the men interviewed were between the ages of 30 and 39, and most had had careers in crime, with their first commitments during their juvenile years. There were almost four times as many property offenders as those who had committed crimes of injury to persons. The majority of the men were released from prison for two to seven years, with about as many out for two to four years as for five to seven. About three- quarters of them had at least a seventh-grade education, and slightly less than half of that group had some high school exposure.

At the outset of the first interview, it did not seem particularly notable that the former inmate wished to make it exceedingly clear that he was not representative of all ex-convicts, but was speaking solely for himself. When most of the ensuing interviews began in the same fashion, it became apparent that each man considered his experiences unique, and one could even get undertones that the ex-convict saw himself as someone special. He would take pride, when supplying background material, in recounting the exploits that had gotten him into trouble with the law. Although the study avoided any question of the continuance of antisocial activity by the participants, and the time elapsed since imprisonment implied that the ex-convict was "going straight," one could not help but feel that an antisocial attitude still prevailed among the respondents. Yet those who participated in the study were especially eager to make suggestions to the interviewer to aid him in obtaining a more accurate picture of the ex-convict and his attitude toward the police. For example, several of the men pointed out that they thought their attitudes would be different from those of ex-convicts who were arrested in big cities. A few who had been arrested elsewhere in the nation said they found the "big-city cop" more impersonal than those at home. This could be true, or it may be that the Eastern City area lawbreaker who is picked up in the big city is not a "regular customer" for that force; his status is not established there, as it is at home. Despite the statements to the contrary, the responses of ex-convicts to the questions posed were relatively uniform.

In answer to the question "How do you feel about cops?" the ex-convict typically expressed an attitude that police officers were doing their jobs when they arrested the respondents, and therefore no hard feelings were harbored. In fact, one respondent answered that if there was one person in the whole correctional system who meant him no harm, it was the policeman. Several men indicated that it is part of the social expectancy of the persistent law violator that he will be beaten by the arresting officer, and that no hard feelings are held. A dominant theme throughout the interviews was that when one becomes a part of the criminal society, the entire process—from the decision to commit a crime to the time when one is released from prison—is all part of a game that contains both punishments and rewards. The policeman is not only expected to beat the criminal, he is even expected to lie in the courtroom in order to get a conviction of the offender. The ex-convict understands that a police officer's promotion depends on arrests and convictions and feels that perjury is therefore justifiable. Detectives need not be as harsh, since they already have status in the department. Westley found in 1957 that the police rationalized their use of violence and other illegal techniques in the apprehension of offenders. The ex-convicts share this rationalization with the police.[12]

What the ex-convict has done is to give an evasive answer to the question about his feelings toward the police and implied through his understanding of police behavior that the relationship is a friendly one. However, the following quotation from Bittner, when read and explained to each of the respondents, elicited a contrary response.

> Moreover, patrolmen find that disciplinary and coercive actions do not affect their friendly relations with the persons against whom these actions are taken. Those who greet and chat with them are the very same men who have been disciplined, arrested, and ordered around in the past, and who expect to be so treated again in the future.[13]

It would seem to be true, as implied by the shared understanding of the role of the policeman and his use of force, and as Bittner in the above quotation has noted, that friendly greeting and chatting shows that a camaraderie exists. Nevertheless, without exception, each of the respondents in the Eastern City area study, with varying degrees of irritation after the reading of the quotation, responded that the police stand aloof from the ex-convict.

A second persistent theme was developed—namely, that the police, just as other correctional personnel, treat the ex-convict as though he were less than human. The irritation arises out of a resentment that although the ex-convict understands and accepts the police officer's punitive behavior, the police officer does not reciprocate with understanding but often responds with derogatory verbal references and beatings designed to be humiliating rather than punishing.

Nothing seems to be more frustrating to the ex-convict than what he believes to be a societal attitude reflected strongly in his interactions with the police, the attitude that he, the ex-convict, is something less than human. This finding was not unexpected. However, when matched with the following quotation from an Eastern City policeman, it shows strikingly that they share an image with the police. When asked why people dislike the police, an answer that was repeated in many ways by several men was best stated by one officer when he said, "Because they [the public] believe we aren't human." Both groups, the ex-convicts and the police, share a negative self-image that precipitates a defensive stance in their daily activities.

In answer to the question "Is your attitude toward cops different from before you were sent up?" most of the men were initially neutral; that is, they indicated that they generally had not thought about the subject before. One only considers "cops" when he is in contact with them. Prodding in this area by asking the respondents to think about the subject now resulted in most of the men's recounting their last experiences with the police. From those who had been out of prison the longest, it produced tales about "bad cops" whom they had known in the past and whom they still avoid.

Although the majority of the men felt that the police paid more attention to them than to the average citizen, they did not appear to believe that the attention constituted "picking on them" or was unwarranted. There was an ambivalence expressed. On the one hand, since they were known to have committed crimes (which they recounted with great relish), they felt that the police had every reason to suspect them and keep them under surveillance. While the societal and police attitudes reported earlier placed them in the "less-than-human" category, that image, which they had internalized, was counteracted by a "superhuman or cunning" self-categorization. What choice did the police have but to use their full powers of detection and surveillance with such people around? On the other hand, they resented police attention because it did reinforce the less-than-human notion and placed undue and unfair attention on them. Their feelings could be summed up as being both proud and resentful of attention by the police, although some seemed to feel that other ex-convicts should definitely be watched. In this last category (those who should definitely be watched) there were strong undertones that the ex-convicts were describing other ex-convicts as members of the less-than-human category that they so thoroughly despised when related to themselves. One ex-convict responded to the question "Should cops keep a close eye on ex-cons?" as follows:

> Yes, they'll repeat most times. We're all crooks. . . . Some guys are just no good all the way. There ain't nuthin' you can do with them. When they get locked up, they should throw away the key. They ain't nuthin' but animals.

Most ex-convicts could and did cite at least one local policeman whom they knew who was brutal in his treatment of ex-convicts. Several men said that these policemen would wait for particular prisoners to be released just to get after them again and that the recently released prisoner would "get the word" that a particular cop was looking for him. With the exception of the brutal and humiliating individual policeman and the allegedly superior attitude of the officer, the ex-convicts considered the police as a group of men dedicated to their job and doing it reasonably well. One could say that their image of the police is possibly more favorable than that held by the public, and that they are certainly more tolerant of illegal procedures sometimes employed by the police.

The older men, who were more likely to have been out of prison the longest and who had less recent and frequent contact with the police than the younger men but who still had contact, claimed that since the Supreme Court decisions of the 1960's, beatings had decreased in number and intensity. The younger men confirmed the story. As one man put it in answer to the questions about when he was stopped last and how he was treated by the arresting officer,

> I've only had two or three beatings (in recent years) and I asked for it. [How?] The last time I was picked up, I was drunk and the cops were shoving me in the front seat of the car. As I slid under the wheel, I saw the keys and tried to start the car. They pulled me out and beat me up. I deserved it.

In answer to the questions requesting their ideas on how they would like to see the police officer change, the ex-convict offered very few suggestions. Some, especially the more articulate ones mentioned early in this chapter, saw the police as the smallest obstacle in the correctional system to the attainment of justice, and looked upon them as a necessary evil. They preferred to discuss other personnel in the correctional system. That was to be expected because of the nature of the *Fortune Society*. All, including the Fortunes, saw the entire process as a game of life in which the police played their part. It is interesting to note that even when the ex-convict talked of those policemen who played their parts poorly (the bad cops), they did not refer to the policemen who stole, took graft, and so on, but to the brutal, humiliating ones.

There are four themes that recur. The first and most dominant theme is frequently implied and occasionally explicitly stated by ex-convicts: crime is a game like any other game. One enters into it with a sense of challenge and excitement that varies from time to time in intensity but is always present. The law violator does not expect to get caught, nor does he usually think of that possibility. He trusts his precautions or his skill in eluding the representatives of the law. If, however, he is caught, he expects to be processed through the correctional system consisting of the police, courts, prisons, and parole. Whatever hardships the correctional agencies impose, especially the prison with all of its resented practices, the ex-convict accepts them as punishments for losing the game. One frequently hears variations of the following statement from prisoners and ex-prisoners: "Don't enter crime unless you're willing to do your time." The ex-convict expects that in the game of crime, which includes crime control, the police may beat him, although this occurs less today than it did before the Supreme Court decisions of the late 1960s. He also expects the police to lie if necessary to obtain a conviction of an offender.

The second theme is that the ex-convicts accept and understand police behavior, with the exception that they are outraged by a feeling that the police consider them to be something less than human. The irony of the situation is that the study of the police showed that they also are agonized by a feeling that they are held to be less than human by the general public. Both groups then, the ex-convicts and the police, share a feeling of oppression, the less-than-human stigma.

The third theme is that the ex-convicts enjoy and resent the extra attention paid to them by the police. The enjoyment derives from their feeling that they are important enough to warrant special attention, and their hostility derives from the stigma attached to being second-class citizens, who are not trusted and free from intrusion upon their privacy.

The fourth and final theme is that the beliefs of the police about the image of them held by ex-convicts are as erroneous as their beliefs about the images of them held by the public in general. Ex-convicts—the bad guys—do not simply dislike the police. They accept police behavior, legal or illegal, as part of the game, but reject the attitude that reflects a gross disdain for the ex-convicts, the less-than-human categorization.

It is unfortunate that the police officer, who craves greater respect and understanding and who shares a minority status with blacks, Spanish-speaking people, and ex-convicts, and other minorities, does not extend to minorities the compassion he wishes for himself. All minority people on either side of the law develop their greatest hostility and are prone to their most belligerent behavior when they are treated "like [lower] animals." A more realistic slogan for the police, and for the society they serve, than those that now are heard would be "humaneness and compassion for humanity!"

Notes

1. For an excellent presentation of this view see Laing, R. D., Phillipson, H., and Lee, A. R., *Interpersonal Perception* (New York: Springer Publishing Co., 1966).

2. Bierstedt, Robert, *The Social Order*, 3d ed. (New York: McGraw Hill Book Co., 1970), p. 468.

3. Skolnick, Jerome H., *Justice without Trial* (New York: John Wiley & Sons, 1967), p. 80.

4. Baldwin, Roger, "Reciprocal Suspicion: Side One," in *Crime, Prevention, and Social Control,* ed. Edward Sagarin and Ronald Akers (New York: Praeger, 1974).

5. Sagarin, Edward, *The Other Minorities* (New York: Ginn and Company, 1971), p. 12.

6. Bayley, David H., and Mendelsohn, Harold, *Minorities and the Police: Confrontation in America* (New York: Free Press, 1969), p. 68.

7. LeMasters, E. E., *Parents in Modern America,* rev. ed. (Homewood, Ill.: Dorsey Press, 1974), p. 91, cites two sources that indicate that 70% of black families have both parents present.

8. Bayley and Mendelsohn, *Minorities and the Police,* p. 66.

9. Baldwin, Roger, "The Police and the Ex-Convict," *Criminology* 8 (Nov. 1970): 279-294.

10. Wilson, J. Q., "Police Morale, Reform, and Citizen Respect: The Chicago Case," in *The Police: Six Sociological Essays,* ed. D. J. Bordua (New York: John Wiley & Sons, 1967).

11. Winslow, R. W., ed., *Crime in a Free Society: Selections from the President's Commission on Law Enforcement and Administration of Justice* (Belmont, Calif.: Dickinson Publishing, 1968), p. 282.

12. Westley, W. A., "Violence and the Police," in *Crime and the Legal Process,* ed. W. Chamblis (New York: McGraw-Hill Book Co., 1968), p. 157.

13. Bittner, E., "The Police on Skid-Row: A Study of Peace Keeping," in *Crime and the Legal Process,* ed. W. Chamblis (New York: McGraw-Hill Book Co., 1968), p. 153.

Chapter **5**

HOW FAR CAN YOU GO?

AT A monthly meeting of the local ministerial group, the discussion turns to dissension among parishioners and society's decreasing respect for the clergy in general. Many reasons are suggested for this unhappy condition. Heated, sincere arguments are generated on many, often unrelated, factors that might play a role in the problem. Little is resolved.

In a setting not very different from the ministerial association's meeting, the teachers' association in the same community decries the lack of respect for teachers from pupils and parents alike. Recognizing how important it is for teachers to obtain the attention of their students and the cooperation of parents, the members proceed to uncover what they believe to be the causes of their problem.

Physicians, too, have come together to determine the reasons for the lack of cooperation on the part of their patients—often extending to the point of jeopardizing their own health.

No group feels more strongly the impact of the lack of respect or the rejection of the authority of its membership than the police department. Perhaps because of their continuous presence in the community and the fact that they are not met at relatively regularly scheduled times and places by persons generally seeking their services, they, more than the other groups, realistically feel more pressure from the societal attitude toward them than the others do. It is difficult enough to experience the rejection of your authority from a parishioner, pupil, or patient who has come to you for services, but it is doubly difficult to receive the rejection when the nature of your occupation places you, the holder of authority, in a relatively continuous but unsought contact with the community of "clients."[1]

The list of occupational groups that are affected by the rejection of their authority by their respective publics can be extended to include any profession or occupational group that strives to attain and maintain professional recognition.[2] Rejection of authority, then, is not just the individual problem faced by a particular occupational group. All these groups are concerned with the rejection of their authority, or their right to perform in particular spheres of activity. The answer to the contemporary problem is contained in the analysis of the concept of authority, its use and abuse by the members of occupational groups, and the resultant societal reactions. The consequences of the overdistension* of authority in the area of police activity are negative reactions by the public, not only to the police officer's misuse of authority but even to his or her proper use of it, weakening the officer's position as an agent of social control and creating a threat to his or her societal image and self-image.

Historically, as societies have become more complex, various tasks have been divided and then subdivided into numerous specializations to deal most effectively with them. The encyclopedists, the generalists, and the "jacks-of-all-trades" of earlier centuries have dwindled down to an exceptional few in all walks of life. Occupational territories have been staked out, fought for, or won by default. It is true that through the process of invention, innovation, and discovery, new territories are continually opened for conquering or acquisition, but they are not of concern to the subject at hand and therefore will not be discussed at length.

---

* Overdistension, as differentiated from overextension, is a more subtle and less conscious process of reaching out into a wider arena of behaviors and activities than originally prescribed.

How does a particular group establish its authority to stake out and claim its exclusive right to practice in an area of work? What do we mean by "authority"? There are the questions that must be dealt with before we can proceed to delineate the dimensions of the overdistension of authority.

Contrary to the statements of the often pained voices of police officials and the rank and file officers who have reached back into their memories of an earlier day to recall that the policeman was highly respected, at no time in the history of American police work was a positive image solidly secure, nor was the social order ever ensured by the presence of the police.

The "watch" originated as a protective device for landowners. They were not overly selective in their appointments of men and were exceedingly parsimonious in the remuneration of their protectors. Therefore, old men, the lame and crippled, and the less employable were sought out (a practice that can still be seen in some smaller American communities today.) In the almost 600 years since the Edict of Winchester required each town to establish its own watch, the general standards for admission to all but the very specialized police forces (FBI, Secret Service, and so on) have not progressed very far. The image of the policeman as someone less than a high-caliber citizen-worker has long historical roots. As Raymond B. Fosdick wrote in *American Police Systems*

> In Philadelphia the difficulty experienced in inducing the citizens to serve their turn as watchmen led to frequent grand jury investigations and presentments. In New York the professional watchmen of the early nineteenth century were objects of constant ridicule; no orgy among young people of the town was complete which did not end up in upsetting a watch-box and its sleeping occupant or in lassoing an unwary "Leatherhead" as he dozed his beat.[3]

In summarizing his findings, Fosdick stated:

> Instead of confidence and trust, the attitude of the public toward the police is far more often than not one of cynicism and suspicion, expressing itself, occasionally, in violent attacks which are as unjust as they are ineffective.[4]

That statement is as valid today as it was in 1921. The distinction between the police as representatives of the law, mobilized to enforce legislation, and the law itself as a body of abstract legislation is often blurred in the eyes of the public. The blame for public disturbances is placed by the social scientific observer on the dislocations of societal structures and processes, but to the general public such disturbances and their weak suppression are attributed to faulty police work. The distrust of the police during the riots in the 1960s is a concrete example of this misunderstanding. Although the behavior of the members of a particular department may have contributed to a disorder, they were not instrumental in causing the disorder. Riot control has long been a weak link in the armament of the police and has contributed to its low image:

> . . . beginning in 1835 a series of mob riots swept the country. A fight in Boston in 1837 between the fire companies and the Irish involved 15,000 persons and was suppressed only by drastic action of militia. In Philadelphia the negro riots of 1838 resulted in the burning of Pennsylvania Hall and the death of many citizens. These riots again broke out in 1842 and negro churches and meeting places were burned. In 1844 the native American riots lasted for three months, during which large numbers of people were killed and wounded and much property, including churches and public buildings were destroyed by the mobs.[5]

It has been shown that the gradual change from a feudal to an industrial form of society led to the institutionalization of a new system of social control for the protection of property and the maintenance of social order. This system from its inception was hampered by a lack of full public support for the development of an efficient, well-paid, and well-trained police organization. Political manipulation and misconceptions of the police as part of the administration rather than as machinery of the law have further reduced their image. Contemporary police systems are outgrowths of the "watch" system, which was part of the changing social structure of England and which was transplanted to

American soil with all its weaknesses. The general public is only vaguely aware, if at all, of the specifics of the history of police systems, and it cannot be claimed that the present image of the police is a rationally conceived outgrowth of the analysis of a sordid police history. In fact, no dominant societal attitude persists because of rational analysis by a total population. Those at a higher socioeconomic and educational level may be slightly more prone toward rational decision making than the other members of society; but, in general, as Sumner has said, folkways and mores change slowly and unconsciously. The attitudes are, if you will, traditionally passed down from generation to generation and are reflected in such phrases as "dumb cops," "crooked cops," and so on. With this background, society has been slow to trust the police and therefore slow in meting out authority to them.

The historical perspective sketched out above is necessary in that it describes the reasons for the cautious extension of authority by the public to police systems. Until quite recently, police organizations have tended to overlook or have chosen to disregard the tentative nature of their authority to the point of its over-distension. We now turn to the concept of authority.

"He is an authority." "He has an authoritarian personality." "She wields a great deal of authority." The term "authority" has several connotations, each of which carries the implication of a high degree of potency. It is an impressive word and therefore is often called into service. The statement "He is an authority" refers to expertise that establishes the person's right to discuss or act in relation to a particular area of knowledge. The phrase "authoritarian personality" connotes a psychological predisposition toward dominance through the ability to coerce others into submission. In the last sentence, an ambiguous statement at best, "authority" may carry the meaning of either of the first two examples, or it may mean social power that has been delegated to the holder, which she may wield upon the group or public with both their acceptance and backing. It is this third definition of authority upon which we must focus in order to understand its use and abuse by police.

Let us examine the concept of authority in more depth before entering into a discussion of its overdistension. Bierstedt has proposed that authority is delegated power, power is implied force, and force is in some way related to actual physical pressure in one form or another.[6] Whereas force is physical coercion, power is the ability to manipulate another or others by the presence or awareness on the part of the respondents of a superior strength or force held by the person in the power position. Power is not a behavior; it is a cognition of the availability of force that is capable of compelling a desired behavior. Authority is synonymous with social power, and social power differs from power alone in that it is not a personal, physical, or psychological characteristic of its holder that compels a particular behavior. Rather, its strength lies in the support of the group, which permits and even urges its holder to assert force with or without their assistance to compel a behavior that they desire. In the words of Simmel, "A super-individual power—state, church, school, family or military organization—clothes a person with a reputation, a dignity, a power of ultimate decision, which would never flow from his individuality."[7] Thus it is that when a person is said to wield authority, in this sense, that person is the representative of a group, given license by that group to bring about or maintain a particular behavior pattern even to the point of using force that they themselves by agreement would not and do not use. The police officer, for example, is the representative of the community, delegated to be the front-line official of its administrative machinery for the maintenance of law and order, who may use physical force even to the extent of using a club or a gun under prescribed circumstances.

Authority relations are often assumed to be totally asymmetrical. Dennis Wrong, in a penetrating article on social power, has examined this exaggerated view and has more accurately stated:

> People exercise mutual influence and control over one another's behavior in all social interactions. . . . Power relations [including authority] are asymmetrical in that the power holder exercises

greater control over the behavior of the power subject than the reverse, but reciprocity of influence—the defining criterion of the social relation itself—is never entirely destroyed except in those forms of physical violence which, although directed against a human being, treat him as no more than a physical object.[8]

And Simmel, the progenitor of these notions on power, has stated, "As a matter of fact, the very feeling of the 'oppressiveness' of authority suggests that the autonomy of the subordinate party is actually presupposed and never wholly eliminated."[9]

The policeman in his uniform, with his badge, gun, and club identifying the outer man, and often with an air of superiority reflected in his gait and demeanor identifying the inner man, exudes authority. The one-sidedness of social interaction with him is eminently clear: he takes command of the situation, whether it be in the role of law officer in the apprehension of an alleged violator or as a peace officer directing traffic or rushing an injured person off to a hospital for treatment. That he is a public servant hired by a governmental agency representing the citizenry is noted only in the futile comments of individual disgruntled citizens who cry "I pay your salary!" Clearly, the advantage in the interaction is heavily weighted in favor of the policeman, as it should be if he is to be effective. He is called upon to make decisions in his role as law officer and peace officer most of his working day. As one author stated,

> The police do prosecutorial work, defense work, judicial work and correctional work. Or put more aggressively, that the policeman exercises a larger judicial discretion than the judge, and that if you are to understand police work you have to recognize the vast range of discretion he has to apply. . . .the police are deciding many more cases than are the judges.[10]

The policeman must decide whether the behavior of a group of boys is extreme enough to require official action, possibly starting the process which will eventuate in labelling one or more boys juvenile delinquents, or whether to bring a drunken husband to the station house to cool off or to be charged with assault, and so on. The policeman recognizes the decision-making function of his position, although he frequently disregards, overlooks, or rejects the limitations imposed upon this privilege or duty.

In an early study of the police image from the policeman's perspective conducted by the author in Eastern City, the responses indicated that policemen felt that the law-abiding public admired them for carrying out the roles of protector, guardian, and decision maker, and that criminals and potential criminals rejected their authority. Their picture was one of "good guys" against "bad guys," but, as Wilson says, "The fact that the policeman can no longer take for granted that noncriminal citizens are also non-hostile citizens may be the most important problem the . . . department must face."[11] That part of the public that supports law and order is also concerned with its rights as citizens (reflected in societal focus on privacy, personal morality, freedom from illegal detention, and so on). They may even challenge the extent of the policeman's discretionary power, asking, for example, whether the police officer has the discretionary power to protect or apprehend one segment of society from a particular behavioral pattern and not another, and how much force is permissible in the process of carrying out his or her duty.

What is the overdistension of authority that police are often accused of? What are the characteristics of overdistension exhibited by any occupational group? Its growth is like that of Topsy: it just happens, and little thought is given to why. Overdistension is a sub-area of overextension.

When a group delegates to a segment of its membership the responsibility for particular activities, it all but relinquishes the rights to performance in those areas. The limited subgroup of members has special status and is expected to perform roles basically unique to them. For example, a church delegates power to its clergy, a school system to its educators, and a society to its physicians. The right to practice in the area of theology is given to the clergy. Others in society may have thoughts about and interests in theological subjects, but the clergy are responsible for theological practice. Each of the occupational groups follows this pattern.

Inherent in the nature of all authority positions is power (delegated). This power is limited to particular areas of responsibility (sometimes referred to as scopes), and there is an expectancy of particular types of performance of the activities. Thus, the clergyman is expected to be the spiritual shepherd, and his congregation expects this to be exhibited in his attendance to all matters pertaining to the church proper, such as church services, visitations, and so on. In return, he may expect the cooperation, attention and respect of his congregation. A frequent development in the self-image of the authority figure is an overestimation of the extent or the boundaries of his powers. He may assume that his leadership is attributable to his personal dominance, or that he can himself determine the boundaries of the power delegated to him. In either case, he extends his efforts into areas that were not included in the original authority contract. For example, the relatively secure minister who because of his sincere, religiously motivated concern marches at the forefront of a protest movement implies (if he wears clerical garb) the support of his church. As an individual citizen, he has a citizen's right (or power) to protest. However, as long as he is in clerical attire, his authority to act is limited or designated by the church; therefore, his excursion into the secular activity is an overdistension. The church may then decide to support him, but prior to and quite possibly after such a march, the election to represent the church was not present. The result may be rejection of the minister if he persists in activities not delegated and not appropriate to the role as defined by the delegating body.

A similar situation can be noted in the educational system when its practitioners extend themselves precariously into therapeutic activities more on the realm of other professionals. Teachers counseling children at length rather than referring them to trained personnel is one example of such overdistension.

One area of activity in which many police departments exhibit overdistension of authority is psychotherapeutic practice, or counseling, by juvenile bureaus and informal counseling of adults (as opposed to referral, which is always a legitimate activity). It has been noted that role conflict occurs between the two legitimate functions of the police, that of peace officer and that of law officer. The additional role of psychotherapeutic counsellor tends to add to that conflict.

The case has been made that police officers are still for the most part undertrained in their primary functions. At this time, when various professional groups are vying for the right to exclusive practice in the subdivisions of the counseling field, the "police therapist" is likely to be regarded as a charlatan for his well-meaning, misplaced efforts. He is resented by his clients, who see his job as being an arresting officer and who are likely to be confused by his dual nature, the second half of which, the "police therapist," appears inappropriate. The general public again, in great part, see such attempts at therapy as "mollycoddling" by a group delegated to arrest the offender. The presence of the professional counsellor or therapist in society tends to confirm the public position that the police agency is not the appropriate source for counseling. The professional counsellor, also, both as a member of the community and through his or her professional associations, resents and rejects the efforts of the police in this area. The assumption of authority to counsel therapeutically is the result not of delegation but of overdistension by police forces. The consequences of such continued activity are that the public generalizes the hostility generated by overdistension into the legitimate areas of activity as well.

Police, like those in Eastern City, are called upon frequently in their peace-keeping roles to do more than physically restrain persons engaged in fighting. They are expected to, and they expect of themselves that they will, leave the scene in quiet, peaceful

Police check sniper report. Boredom from the everyday routine patrol ends with a thunderous crash and the report of a sniper shooting from a window in an otherwise quiet and peaceful neighborhood. (Bethlehem Police Dept., Bethlehem, Pa.)

order. The incongruity of the situation is that the community does not recognize the skills necessary for the officer to carry out this function and he or she, too, even when exposed to various programs such as crisis-intervention training, thinks all it takes is "a little common sense" to straighten things out. Eastern City has recently instituted crisis training as part of its regular recruit training program; but in the recruits' evaluation of their training, the courses in the areas of human relations rated low in their estimation.[12] Yet in a short time they will be called upon to deal with human-relations problems. Ironically, some of them will volunteer for those positions mentioned earlier that place them in the role of police therapist. The Chief of Eastern City Police once commented that it was not so much that he and his men did not know the boundaries, since they were defined by law; it was more that the lawmakers, themselves, expected the police to overdistend themselves in problem situations. If things did not go well after each overextension, the politicians were covered by referring to their legislation rather than to their unofficial prodding for action. In some of the more advanced or forward-looking departments around the nation, the problem of overdistension in the area of counseling is dissipated either by a very extensive and intense training program or by hiring psychotherapists to be on call. These practices have the dual effect of creating a greater respect for the police by professional therapists who work with them (a respect reciprocated by the police) and, more importantly, a changed public attitude toward the police role in counseling, or simply a legitimization by the community of a police activity that was once overdistensive.

In the 1950s, the policeman enjoyed the relative stability of a society recently mobilized militaristically to defend itself from aggressors. It consisted of many returned veterans resentful of, but accustomed to, a high degree of authoritarianism. Much of the population could be and was described by social critics as apathetic. The 1960s and 1970s have been a period of great fluidity and structural changes. Traditional social institutions have been threatened or torn down. New ones, mostly of an experimental nature, have emerged. Civil-rights legislation and programs, social-welfare agencies and institutions on a massive scale, and educational programs in hallowed institutions have been questioned; the tidy structures of family and religion are no longer secure from questioning. And, somewhere in the middle of these dislocations of social structure stands the police officer, relatively untrained, underpaid, suffering from low morale, attempting to carry out his role of decision maker and/or protector and guardian of the law on the streets or front line of the community. The major policy makers, the governmental officials, are themselves frequently overwhelmed with the tasks of decision making. And whereas these officials may have built-in mechanisms in the political machinery for "buck passing," delaying, or avoiding the issues, the police officer is confronted with issues that demand immediate solutions.

Without the clearcut direction of a governmental organization in his or her numerous activities, the police officer quite frequently must decide matters alone. As a member of a quasi-military organization, authoritarian in structure, with the boundaries of discretionary authority loosely defined or undefined, the officer's priority is to act strongly; in doing so, he or she frequently overdistends his or her authority. "The unwarranted use of authority toward citizens includes a variety of charges relative to the employment of illegal means such as the undue use of force and threats, harassment, uncivil treatment through abusive language and demeaning epithets, and the application of illegal means in investigation, e.g., illegal search and seizure of evidence."[13] A second choice the officer sometimes makes, mainly because of sensitivity to public approval, or at least an awareness of being in the public eye, is not to act at all in order to avoid an incident. In the first instance, we see the "head beater" in the gathering crowd or potential-riot situation. In the second instance, we see the policeman of the 1960s standing by as shops are looted in a ghetto-area riot and of the early 1970s standing by as hundreds of youths crash the gates at rock concerts. The policeman is found guilty in these scenes of commission and omission; in both, he has overextended his weakly defined authority as protector and guardian of the public order. He reacts to the lack of support from his local government, which does not clearly define his responsibilities. He also reacts to people who reject his solutions to the maintenance of order. There is a great deal of griping within the department, and cries for a stronger and more militant Fraternal Order of Police. Occasionally splinter groups of militant policemen are organized, which threaten segments of the public in word and deed.

The results of the hostility within police departments just described is that the police as an in-group see the public as an out-group; or, if you prefer, the police, as a minority group, see the wider society as a hostile enemy to be dealt with by the means that they know best and are legitimately least allowed to use—force. The consequences are that the out-group—actually consisting of many groups—not only rejects the activities of the police that are not clearly defined, but also distrusts and rejects their authority even when they are performing duties that are legitimately recognized.[14]

The role of the policeman in the riot situation has been alluded to and two of his alternatives described. He may either be precipitous and abuse his authority, as noted in the reference to "head beaters," or he may stand aside. He is damned if he does and damned if he doesn't! The out-group widens and strengthens with either response.

Another area directly related to the policeman's overuse of authority is the discriminatory treatment of the alleged offender. "This discretionary role, however, has not been explicitly sanctioned by society (nor even by command within the department). Since the police lack guidelines for the exercise of their discretionary function, citizens question the criterion on which they do exercise it . . . i.e., social class rather than wrongdoing determines whether a citizen will attract the attention of the police."[15] For many years, police departments have used one form of questioning for those of the middle and upper classes and another for the lower classes. Documentation of the process known as "the third degree" is not difficult to find in the literature. Advising clients of their legal rights was also done in varying degrees depending on class or status, although it must be said that knowledge of their rights and therefore the appearance of legal representation for the middle and upper classes resulted more from the knowledge they already had than from guidance by police officials. Nevertheless, imparting different amounts of information according to class and status was an abuse of power and of the

Setting up a training schedule. The police have not been especially happy about Supreme Court decisions that they interpret as favoring the criminal and limiting police power. Trying to interpret to officers the meaning of such decisions and new techniques of police work in a few brief sessions is next to futile. (Robert Reier)

responsibility to afford protection to all, including the alleged offender, whatever his class might be.

One consequence of this form of abuse of authority has been legislation that clearly defines the rights of all individuals. One can interpret such legislation as meaning that the society is supporting the police agencies by producing the much-needed and requested direction or assignment of authority; or one can, as many of the police have done, interpret such legislation as a means of limiting and hampering the authority of the police. Both interpretations are possible. Legislation on such matters as interrogation, rights to counsel, and wiretapping define the limits of authority and at the same time restrict the policeman from doing the job as he has traditionally perceived it.

The overdistension of authority has caused numerous elements of the population to see the police as incompetent or abusive. The police officer has reacted by either using force or taking no action

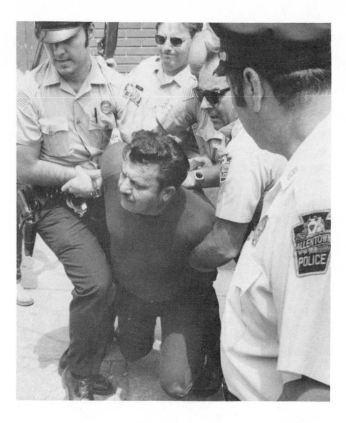

Restraining a suspect. Single-handed heroics in the difficult job of restraining a suspect are not the norm, TV notwithstanding. Seasoned police officers see most TV police shows as fantasy. (Call-Chronical Newspapers, Allentown, Pa.)

at the scene, by internalizing the problem within his fraternal organization, and occasionally by striking out militantly. The discriminatory use of authority in relation to the alleged offender has resulted in legislation to define and limit police powers. In both instances, the image of the police has suffered, morale has been lowered, and the relative efficiency of police departments as effective agents of social control has been weakened.

Is all lost? Has our system of police services, as structured, outlived its utility? The answer needs to be seen in relation to the total social scene. One could ask the same questions about other agencies within the social institutions of contemporary society that also are under the scrutiny of our society. Have politics, religion, education, the family, and their many agencies of administration outlived their utility? No one really seems to be stating that they have. That they need to be examined and restructured in the light of contemporary knowledge and value systems is the cry of today, and police systems have come to the forefront for scrutiny if for no other reason than that the overdistension of authority has frequently called attention to them.

Notes

1. As many parents of young children can testify, father as the household disciplinarian has an easier position than mother who, because of her constant presence, must mete out discipline throughout the day.

2. Etzioni, Amitai, *Modern Organizations* (Englewood Cliffs, N.J.: Prentice-Hall, 1964). Etzioni refers to such striving groups as "quasi-professional."

3. Fosdick, Raymond B., *American Police Systems* (New York: The Century Co., 1921), p. 61.

4. Ibid., p. 380.

5. Ibid., pp. 65-66.

6. Bierstedt, Robert, "The Problem of Authority," in *The Study of Society,* ed. Peter I. Rose (New York: Random House, 1967), pp. 603-614.

7. Wolff, Kurt H., ed., *The Sociology of Georg Simmel* (New York: Free Press, 1950), p. 184.

8. Wrong, Dennis, "Some Problems in Defining Social Power," *American Journal of Sociology* 73 (May 1968): 673.

9. Wolff, *The Sociology of Georg Simmel.*

10. Morris, Norval, "Politics and Pragmatism in Crime Control," *Federal Probation,* June 1968, p. 13.

11. Wilson, James Q., "Police Morale, Reform, and Citizen Respect: The Chicago Case," in *The Police: Six Sociological Essays,* ed. David J. Bordua (New York: John Wiley & Sons, 1967), p. 158. See Chapter 4, "Whom Do You Trust?" for ex-cons' views about police.

12. See Chapter 2, "South Side—Downtown," on the education of police officers.

13. Some of the out-group are Negro militants, nonviolent Negroes and whites, and relatively liberal or conservative nonactivist whites.

14. Reiss, Albert J., Jr., *The Police and the Public* (New Haven: Yale University Press, 1971), p. 141.

15. Gamire, Bernard I., Rubin, Jesse, and Wilson, James Q., *The Police and the Community* (Baltimore: Johns Hopkins University Press, 1972), p. 36.

Chapter **6**

THE OFFICIAL PEEKING ORDER

POLICEMEN take every opportunity, in private discussion or on public platforms, to talk about the Gault and Miranda decisions.[1] And, while they insist that the laws of the land must be respected and obeyed, they decry the situation that Supreme Court decisions of the 1960s have left them. The right to counsel and the extension of constitutional rights to children, who until such decisions were made often confessed or were made to confess to delinquent acts, seem to be considered an infringement on their "rights" by the police.

In the instance of riots, the police have modified the nature of their response to community disturbances at which their duty compelled them to appear. In the second instance, it has been their own, nonduty, voluntary response to frustrating court decisions that has helped to modify the police image. Through a series of televized and written reports, the public has witnessed the functioning of the police and has responded—sometimes favorably and at other times not. The society and the police themselves have both questioned the proper functions of the "men and women in blue."

The nature of the "new morality" is a more complex and unclear subject than the nature of police functions. It may be summed up as society's view of the importance of the individual's right to decision making, which pervades all aspects of life, or in a phrase of the 1960s, "doing one's thing." It involves an intense reaction to any form of regulation that would impinge upon the individual's private thoughts or behavior. Strangely enough, to protect these freedoms of thought and private action, a loose but observable unity of expression has emerged, especially in the younger and predominantly liberal ranks of the population. As in the case of the police, the news media—such as television, newspapers, and magazines—and college textbooks all have increased their coverage of the subject of morality, particularly with regard to the question of sexual freedom. In the following pages we shall explore the subject of the forced "marriage" of police functions and sexual freedom and their family of conflicts.

In 1937, in an analysis of the functions of government, Robert MacIver very sagely noted that the state can control people's morality in a very limited way at best and suggested that attempts at limitation are foolish and ridiculous. Speaking of such attempts, he observed, "We have entered a sphere in which mere enforcement is futile." He goes on to say that the feelings of people can be controlled only by themselves, through an internal authority "to which the compulsive state cannot aspire."[2] If the members of a society delegate authority to the state to control morality, then they must also provide adequate means of enforcing the laws they make. The only enforceable laws are those dealing with public behavior. If there were any doubt at the time of MacIver's writing that societal agreement and support of governmental restrictions on private sexual morality existed, there can be little doubt today that the direction of public opinion tends toward the opposite pole. Without such support, existing legislation loses much of its force and is regularly violated. The police, as agents of the government directed to enforce the laws, are faced with the problems of insufficient manpower, inadequate training (with regard to proper techniques of detection and apprehension that do not violate individual rights), and controversy at all levels of government regarding the relevance of such laws. These problems result in incomplete support by government officials and magistrates for police action; in societal ambivalence, heavily weighted against police action; and in the ambivalence of the police toward both the laws and the morality of the acts involved.

Herbert L. Packer, a noted legalist, contends that the diversity of the American people is the source of the difficulty in legislating public morality. Regarding the function of the police, he states, "There is simply no way for the police to provide so much as a semblance of enforcement of laws against prostitution, sexual deviance . . . without widespread and visible intrusion into what people regard as their private lives."[3] Skolnick and Woodworth, in a study of a police department's morals detail, concur with Packer's view and write, "It does not matter very much if criminal law forbids various erotic activities, so long as it is impossible to see through walls. . . . Even among the police themselves, therefore, the norms of the changing process vary with the differences in police attitudes toward sexual morality. . . . Most important perhaps is a persistent theme mixing elements of sexual interest, jealousy, and revulsion."[4]

The United States more than any other Western society has maintained a commitment to the Judeo-Christian ethic concerning sexual expression. This ethic is reflected in the laws of the land and reinforced in the doctrines of the organized churches. Of the two institutions that perpetuate the ethic, government and religion, the one that might be expected to be most resistant to change in what are basically religious precepts, the church, is the more flexible. A few years ago, the term "sex" would have been taboo in religious discussions. Today, sex is not only being discussed openly but is also a major subject of the clergy's pastoral conselling programs. The Pill and other contraceptives have greatly reduced the threat of unwanted pregnancy. Abortion removes it. Medicines for venereal diseases have reduced their threat to life, and psychology, especially of the psychoanalytical orientation, has permitted modern people to see sexual activity as a healthy expression of human nature rather than as sinful and unclean. Even the Roman

Catholic church, the strongest hold-out from revising its position on sexual matters, is experiencing pressure to change. Though the predominant position prevails, its lay and clerical membership contains many who are strongly advocating change to the Vatican.

It is impossible to state with any degree of certainty just how much change has occurred in actual sexual behavior patterns in the history of American society. Phrases such as "the sexual revolution" and "the new morality" are deceptively simple. It is more likely that Ira Reiss's discovery regarding sexual permissiveness with affection by females is not recent in origin; the double standard followed by males was never a tightly guarded secret.[5] The current mode of thinking asserts that sex is a personal, private, most intimate matter, to be governed by conscience and not by legislation. Sex, this position holds, should be free of religious or legal guilt.

However, legislation pertaining to sexual activity remains relatively unchanged. Most states retain laws against fornication and adultery. Fornication charges are rarely, if ever, presented in court, and adultery charges are usually brought up in divorce and not criminal suits. With the exception of rape laws, which have become more stringent after a series of shocking occurrences, most sex laws remain unchanged.

The two overall functions of the police are the *enforcement of criminal law* and the *maintenance of public order*. In the first instance, the police act as *law officers;* and in the second, as *peace officers.* The amount of time spent as a peace officer is greater than the amount of time spent in catching alleged criminals; therefore, the officer's major role-behavior should be that of a friend. But the policeman himself and the general society see him predominantly as a foe of wrongdoers.[6] This image interferes with his peace-keeping duties, since as a foe he brings with him a suspicious, hostile, and blatantly forceful manner. Only in the limited amount of interaction within dangerous criminal situations is that image appropriate. "The point is that the situations in which the police officers most frequently find themselves do not require the expert aim of a marksman, the cunningness of a private eye, or the toughness of a stereotyped Irish policeman. Instead, they demand knowledge of human beings and the personal, as opposed to official, authority to influence people without the use or even threat of force."[7]

The public's increasingly hostile attitude toward the official morals enforcers, the police, together with the changing sex norms and the unchanging laws, complicate the issue of maintaining a public moral order. Part of the hostility reflects the resentment of the officer as the person who represents the law to the public, part arises from the manner of detection, and part stems from the generalized public hostility toward the foe image.

After establishing the wider issues that disturb society, having presented in general form the nature of the moral and legal dilemmas surrounding sexual activity, and having summarized the background with which the police enter the arena of moral-code enforcement, we shall now observe some of the specific sexual practices that are legally prohibited because they are alleged to give offense to the society and that evoke police action.

The acts of child molestation and forcible rape will be omitted from the examination, not because they are not illegal and offensive, but because they evoke the least disagreement on the part of the public over the need for code enforcement and the efforts toward arrests by the police. A case could be made for the review of the treatment of child molesters, or one on victim-precipitated rape, but in both instances capture and arrest are widely supported.[8]

The types of sex offenses that are affected by the changing norms of society and in turn shape societal attitudes as well as, to some lesser extent, police attitudes toward arrest include prostitution, homosexuality, statutory rape, fornication, and adultery. What is common to all of these offenses is that they are acts that are agreed upon by both parties before they are committed. With some notable exceptions in the areas of homosexuality and prostitution, all of these acts are ones in which

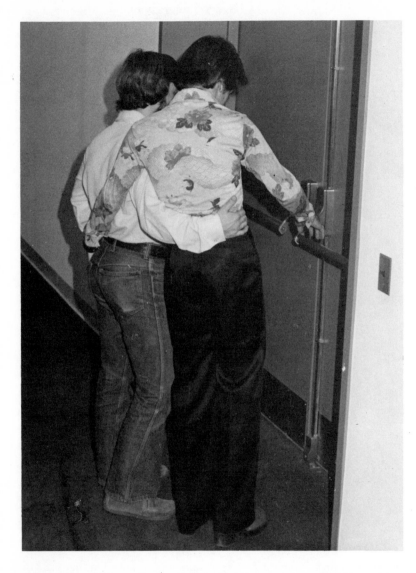

Brotherly love? The policeman's masculinity means appearing big and tough. Homosexuals often reflect the reverse of this image. To the policeman they are, therefore, people to be held in great disdain, frequently to be harassed, if not arrested. (Robert Reier)

C'm'ere a minute. Not only can prostitutes be tolerated, but they can also be useful as sources of information. As long as they cooperate with the police and do not indulge in felonious action (such as mugging or rolling a "John"), they are not likely to be arrested in many cities. (Robert Reier)

the "victim" can also be labeled the offender.[9] As noted earlier, fornicators and adulterers are not actively pursued and prosecuted by enforcement agencies and will be omitted from discussion, although their relevance is understood. Statutory rape involves consenting partners at least one of whom is below a legally defined age. Were they older, they would be dealt with (or not) as fornicators. The primary question is, at what age are young persons capable of making their own decisions? The various states establish arbitrary age limits, and by dint of the accident of birthdate, the person(s) involved will be either taken into custody or simply ignored, or at most given an unheeded warning not to repeat the act. Skolnick and Woodworth have aptly noted that, for example, at the age of 19 (in some states) a young woman is responsible for her behavior, although at 18 she may be quite knowing and aware. The age difference determines whether she is considered a saint or a slut.[10] The two sexual offenses that receive the most surveillance by the police, and that will therefore be the principal examples in the remainder of this chapter, are prostitution and homosexuality.

Three major questions arise in a discussion of the proper role of the police as protectors of public morality. First, the problem of police intervention is confused by the question of whether a sexual act performed publicly or in complete privacy by two mature, consenting persons is under some circumstances a violation of public morality and at other times not. According to present law the answer is usually "yes." The tide of current opinion is that police intervention in a mutually agreed-upon sexual activity is simply meddling in the private lives of citizens. A second, and perhaps more difficult, problem with which police are faced is the question of whether their methods are more than just interfering and involve the police to a great extent as participants in the illegal act. Is an act legal when committed by a police officer in the line of duty and illegal when engaged in by ordinary citizens? Lastly, is police action and any ensuing legal process an effective deterrent to the alleged crime? Packer answers these questions by saying,

"Whether the locale is a lover's lane, a national park, a city street, or a wild party at someone's house, the criminal law should have no concern with consensual sexual conduct unless the trier of fact can say that the conduct took place under circumstances which created a substantial risk that someone might be offended." And as for deterrence, he says, "The whole tedious, expensive, degrading process of enforcement-activity produces no results: no deterrence, very little incapacitation, and certainly no reform."[11]

The police officers, and especially members of their own families, question the double standard that prevails both within and outside the line of duty. Several wives of police officers interviewed at length for Chapter 3 of this book responded quite negatively to the idea of having their husbands on the vice squad. The opportunity for illicit relations is greater in the areas that their husbands patrol, and the techniques applied to catch offenders in the act are distressing, if not threatening, to some wives. One wife commented, "I don't want . . . making up to those queens and I certainly don't want him in bed with no [sic] other women!" In the line of duty or not, wives are not fond of having their husbands "messing around." Still another wife of a patrolman not on the vice squad, discussing the sexual behavior of men in the department, asked the author, "Did you hear about the big scandal at . . . Hospital several years ago? Three married policemen having affairs; two with nurses and one with the night supervisor? . . . Did you know about the policeman who was discovered in the back of a panel truck parked on a city street in a very embarrassing situation with a woman? He is now a lieutenant and never a month goes by that his name isn't in the local press. He goes around lecturing to women's organizations for the police department. It makes me sick!"

It is oversimplified to respond to the stories cited above and many more like them, reported mainly by family members rather than the men themselves (with a few exceptions), with statements such as that there are always a few "bad cops" on the force or that "all cops" are "on the make and on the take." The police are members of the same society that they are employed to protect, with the same strengths and weaknesses. When they appear to put themselves above the rest of society by not using the same rules of enforcement on their membership, the police image is tarnished.

On the surface it would appear that the police officer's job in a morals case or in any other type of offense would be a relatively simple one of enforcing the laws and ordinances in his or her own jurisdiction. Questions concerning changing morality or the injustice of particular legislation are technically beyond the sphere of control of the police. The officer does not determine law, he or she enforces it. Officers' social class and educational background serve to undergird their usually conservative and dogmatic stance, a position that partially relieves them from the social pressures involved in questioning the appropriateness of their actions. Yet, their membership in the wider society and the range of discretion permitted them by the seemingly precise definitions of criminal offenses do not shield them from the decision-making process.[12]

Since the removal of the policeman from the beat and the advent of specialized units, the primary responsibility for catching sex offenders is vested in the vice squad or morals detail. Members of this unit consider themselves experts in a highly specialized area of police detection. They also see their position as one that produces little favorable recognition and much scorn. Their rewards must be derived from personal satisfactions at beating the system and at upholding their own interpretations of the law, thereby serving the cause of "true justice."

As the author was gathering data through discussion with vice-squad members, an officer related the following story. As part of his regular duties, one of his stakeouts was at a public rest station near a college campus. Each day, he would spend several hours in or near the facility. Most days, when he finished that part of his tour of duty and walked toward his car, students from the college, recognizing him from his daily appearances, would yell to him, "Goodbye, Homo." While relating the story, he said good-naturedly and with a forced smile that he always got a good laugh from the students' remarks; but clearly he was agitated by the implication that he, with his high standards of morality, could be thus labeled and that he could not respond and reveal his true identity. His only reward, he explained, came not from public support but from satisfaction that he was keeping the rest station free from degenerates who might prey upon an unsuspecting public.

The vice squad is committed to the "crime-control model" as differentiated from the "due-process model" of law. In the "due-process model," the emphasis is on the determination of legal guilt, and conforming to legal technicality runs through the entire process. In the "crime-control model," the establishment of factual guilt and the attempt to prosecute the greatest number of offenders, thereby decreasing or controlling the problem, are the goals.[13] Policemen see it as their duty to ferret out sex offenders and to use whatever means are available to prevent repetition of the offending behavior. They are constantly frustrated not only by the attitudes of the public toward them but also by the judicial process. If a judge in his or her use of the due-process model releases an alleged offender on what the officer considers a meager technicality, or if another judge takes the position that the offense is not as serious as the arresting officer considers it to be, then the officer is less likely to use the courts as the means of control in the future and will resort to other methods. Whether the officer attempts to use a policy of "(1) complete repression, (2) formal and open segregation, or (3) . . . nominal repression accompanied by tacit segregation and regulation," the primary method of control in lieu of judicial proceedings is some form of harrassment.[14] He may, for example, detain and question a prostitute knowing full well that he has no intention of bringing the case to court. His purpose, as he sees it, is to annoy the "harlot."

Approaching prostitutes and homosexuals, engaging them in a way that leads to a solicitation from them, and then harassing them is part of the process involved in beating the systems. The systems beaten are the sex offenders' patterns of evading detection and the judicial process, which may often release offenders who are caught in the act of soliciting or engaging in illegal activity.

The policeman's hostility toward the prostitute is not as great as that which he harbors against the homosexual. He is ambivalent about the prostitute's behavior; he finds the homosexual's behavior repulsive. He sees the prostitute from a moralistic standpoint as evil and unclean and from a legalistic position as a law violator whose activities often extend into other illegal channels such as narcotics addiction or various forms of larceny. Yet, if she remains relatively discreet in her trade and limits herself to prostitution, he sees her as providing a service to weak men. Under the usually unwritten rules of the double standard, arrests —if they are made at all—are usually of the prostitutes only.

Often the prostitute's customers are well-known members of the community, and one of the officer's satisfactions is "knowing" that he is a better man than the weak community leader. Promotions are frequently dependent upon politics, both within and outside of the department. The vice-squad member somehow often finds himself more likely to have political advantage than members of other units of the force. His policy of arrests reveals his wide discretionary powers and his personal biases. Unless forced to do so by his superiors, he will not arrest prostitutes who keep him informed of the activities and whereabouts of other prostitutes in his area. He will almost always arrest prostitutes who solicit customers of a different race, and he is most likely to arrest prostitutes who have not been "cleared" by his informants. He will usually follow a course of outwardly appearing to repress prostitution while permitting it to occur in certain parts of the city under rules he creates. If the policeman believes that he is not in full control of his territory because of noncooperation from the prostitutes, or if a drive toward elimination of prostitution is directed from higher authorities, then he will resort, at least temporarily, to a policy of complete repression—which, of course, is never fully carried out.

Working on the vice squad is a cat-and-mouse game. The policeman knows where his prey is most likely to be found. He stealthily approaches the prostitute; he occasionally misses her, thereby whetting his appetite; and when he has her in his clutches, he then decides whether to toy with her by harassment or to attempt to devour her in the legal process. Although the statutes differ from state to state, most of the arrests take place in the act of solicitation.[15] The policeman, until he is well known in the area, will often play the role of a customer seeking to be solicited. He makes it as clear as possible without mentioning price that he is willing to pay. The woman, in a self-protective manner, attempts to set her price indirectly. She may speak, for example, of a need for money for a "poor, old mother" but not state a price for her "services." Once the officer has received a price for sexual activity and possibly paid for it in marked bills, he makes the arrest. His decision to bring the case to court may be based on his own spot judgment of the woman's character and his expectation of court cooperation. If he decides to permit the woman to continue her activity discreetly and under his surveillance, then action will not be taken. If he believes that the court will prosecute the case to his satisfaction, then he will bring her to court so that the woman will stop her activities. If he believes that the court will not prosecute her effectively, then he may subject the woman to temporary incarceration, interrogation, and a physical examination purely for their harassing effect. The prostitute expects harassment or occasional court appearances as part of the game, but if various members of the vice squad or outside decoys are successful in apprehending her several times in a short span of time, she may decide to leave the area, and that policeman has won his battle.[16]

Harassment clearly is a nonlegal technique included in the policeman's operating skills for the control of prostitution and other sex offenses. Encouragement and entrapment are two other techniques, which are not so easily defined and which evoke defensive responses when discussed with policemen. "Encouragement," the less offensive term and practice, is more readily justified by those who would recommend the use of either. "Entrapment," like many legal terms, varies in meaning from state to state. Entrapment differs from encouragement in that the officer solicits the illegal activity rather than merely making himself unmistakably available for solicitation. From a legal point of view, it would appear that under certain circumstances one or the other technique might be considered appropriate police action. The basic support for these practices arises from the fact that detection of sex offenses is more difficult than detection of some other types of law violations. It is expected in nonsex cases that there are many instances in which the police may have to resort to undercover work in order to dredge up information necessary to make arrests of dangerous criminals. Prostitution, however, except in cases in which street walkers aggressively accost men who may be highly offended (but not placed in danger), is usually a covert activity carried out by two consenting partners in private. Neither partner can be described as a dangerous criminal. Whether it be encouragement or entrapment that is employed to dupe a prostitute into solicitation, it is carried out in such a way so as to create the setting for a private, personal, intimate act, and is therefore essentially an invasion of privacy (or, more accurately, an invasion of private morality). Discovering a bona fide customer and a prostitute after they have agreed to or are performing sexual acts is more readily seen as an invasion of privacy because both partners have entered into a private, covert contract. The answer to the question of whether a policeman should make an arrest in either case will have to come either from a change in the laws to reflect the changing sex mores of society or from a wider use of the policeman's discretionary power in arrests.

In the final analysis of the subject of prostitution, as Packer states, "There seems little reason to believe that the incidence of prostitution has been seriously reduced by criminal law enforcement although the forms in which it is conducted have altered."[17]

Just as in prostitution, the "victim" of the homosexual, with the exception of the young child accosted by an aggressive homosexual, is a willing one. He or she is unlikely to prosecute a sex partner. This is especially true when both partners are homosexuals, possibly living in a love relationship, or members of an intimate circle of participants. The partner solicited in either a public or private facility is also unlikely to reveal the homosexual's identity to the police, since he or she would be incriminated as well.

A most significant problem that confounds the question of police enforcement of morality is whether a sexual act performed in private but agreed upon in a public place is a private or public act. If the place where the act was agreed upon is the determining criterion, then the act is a public one; but if the place where the act was performed was in seclusion and is the determining factor, then it was a private act. The issue is further complicated by the question of whether any sexual act agreed upon in a private discussion by two people anywhere is not in essence private in all instances.

The police, as described earlier, often spend a great amount of time in public rest rooms or other places where they expect to find homosexuals. They will be suspicious of anyone loitering in a public rest room. Some officers will be suggestive verbally or expose themselves in front of a urinal for extended periods of time in order to entice a homosexual into making a proposition. In answer to questions about the possibility of enticing someone who otherwise might not have had the courage or desire to make a proposition, the officers' answer is that it makes no difference. They believe that the purpose that the individual had in mind when he entered the rest room was homosexual activity, and that whether enticed or aggressive, the homosexual must be caught and removed. Policemen do not see their own behavior as improper, even though it would be considered indecent exposure if committed by others. It is to them simply a necessary technique for capturing offenders.

It should be noted that neither policemen nor policewomen are prone to actively seek out female homosexuals, or lesbians. The latter are less likely to be noticed, as females are permitted by society a wider latitude than males in their overt sexual embraces. They simply are not suspected or even found to be as repulsive as males might be. In addition, "There exists in most societies, as in our own, a dearth of laws relating specifically to female homosexuality."[18]

It is doubtful that the policeman's harassment of the male homosexual would subside if legislation were changed; and, as Packer has suggested, it is also unlikely that homosexuality would increase if legislation were rescinded. The social stigma attached to homosexuality by society and notably by members of law enforcement agencies already must be and would continue to be a deterrent to some potential homosexuals. Those whose urges are more powerful, whatever their origin, would continue with or without legislation.[19] If anything, with the current visibility of homosexual organizations, police repression is no deterrent.

The policeman is not concerned with academic debates over whether homosexuality is the product of heredity, environment, or both. To the officer, the homosexual is a degenerate, something less than a male. This is especially important to the policeman who is acutely conscious of maleness, and most are.

In this chapter we have excluded discussions of topics such as forcible rape or pedophilia because legislators, society in general, and the police in particular are in some agreement that the offenders should be apprehended and treated or punished. Fornication and adultery were reviewed in a cursory manner because the behavior of police in such offenses is in accord with the sentiments of the general population, though not with current legislation. The police rarely apprehend violators in these two categories. Therefore, prostitution and homosexuality were used as the primary examples of police activity with sex offenders.

It is strikingly clear in the major examples that the powers of the police in decision making concerning sex offenses is as great in impact as, if not greater than, the legal and judicial processes. That is, the police use a significant amount of discretion in determining how serious they consider a particular act to be, how they will proceed to apprehend the offender, and what means of deterrence they will employ, regardless of the laws or the judicial apparatus available. In cases such as forcible rape, prostitution accompanied by narcotics offenses or "rolling" a customer, or any act performed by coercion, the action of the police is supported by public attitude. Public support diminishes but does not disappear when the sexual offender is aggressive and commits an act in a public place. For example, indecent exposure, petting in a "lovers' lane," or soliciting in barrooms or rest rooms can be, and is often described as, offensive to some members of society, especially to those who may be solicited. Public support wanes when it is the police who use aggressive tactics. When the police resort to methods of detection that involve them in acts that if committed by others would be illegal, and in which no dangerous criminal is to be apprehended, then their behavior is considered inappropriate and distasteful. When the act involves consenting partners and is performed in privacy, police intervention is considered offensive and humiliating and serves neither positive nor practical purposes. However strong the current attitude about the private nature of sexual acts, the police, without further guidance, training, or directives, will continue to exert wide discretionary powers as morals enforcers.

Notes

1. *Gault* v. *United States* (1967) extended rights to youth, and *Miranda* v. *Arizona* (1966) required police to state the right to counsel to suspects before interrogation.

2. MacIver, Robert M., *Society: A Textbook of Sociology* (New York: Farrar & Rinehart, 1937), p. 292.

3. Packer, Herbert L., *The Limits of the Criminal Sanction* (Stanford, Calif.: Stanford University Press, 1968), p. 283.

4. Skolnick, Jerome H., and Woodworth, J. Richard, "Bureaucracy, Information, and Social Control: A Study of a Morals Detail," in *The Police: Six Sociolgical Essays,* ed. David Bordua (New York: John Wiley & Sons, 1967), pp. 101, 115, 120.

5. *See* Kinsey, Alfred C., Pomeroy, Wardell B., and Martin, Clyde E., *Sexual Behavior in the Human Male* (Philadelphia: W. B. Saunders, 1948); Kinsey, Alfred C. et al., *Sexual Behavior in the Human Female* (Philadelphia: W. B. Saunders, 1953); Reiss, Ira L., *The Social Context of Premarital Sexual Permissiveness* (New York: Holt, Rinehart & Winston, 1967) and others for an elaboration of this view of contemporary attitudes toward sex.

6. See Chapter 5.

7. Terris, Bruce J., "The Role of the Police," *The Annals* 374 (November 1967): p. 67.

8. *See* McCaghy, Charles H., "Child Molesters: A Study of Their Careers as Deviants," in *Criminal Behavior Systems, A Typology,* ed. Marshall D. Clinard and Richard Quinney (New York: Holt, Rinehart & Winston, 1967), pp. 75-87; Schafer, Stephen, *The Victim and His Criminal* (New York: Random House, 1968).

9. *See* Schur, Edwin, *Crimes without Victims* (Englewood Cliffs, N.J.: Prentice-Hall, 1965).

10. Skolnick and Woodworth, "Bureaucracy, Information, and Social Control," p. 132.

11. Packer, *The Limits of the Criminal Sanction,* p. 311 and p. 329.

12. *See* Skolnick, Jerome H., *Justice without Trial* (New York: John Wiley & Sons, 1966). The entire book is about the police and decision making.

13. *See* Skolnick, ibid., Chapter 9, and Packer, Herbert L., "The Two Models of the Criminal Process," *University of Pennsylvania Law Review* 113 (November 1964): 1-68.

14. Lemert, Edwin M., "Prostitution," in *Problems of Sex Behavior,* ed. Edward Sagarin and Donal E. F. MacNamara (New York: Thomas Y. Crowell Co., 1968), p. 92.

15. Tiffany, Lawrence P., McIntyre, Donald M., Jr., and Rotenberg, Daniel L., *Detection of Crime* (Boston: Little, Brown, 1967), p. 214.

16. *See* Skolnick and Woodworth, "Bureaucracy, Information, and Social Control," for specific cases of harassment.

17. Packer, *The Limits of the Criminal Sanction,* p. 328.

18. Kirkham, George L., "The Female Homosexual," in *Critical Issues in the Study of Crime,* ed. Simon Dinitz and Walter C. Reckless (Boston: Little, Brown, 1969), pp. 190-194.

19. Packer, *The Limits of the Criminal Sanction,* p. 302.

Chapter 7

MORALE, THE KEY TO SOLUTIONS

NO ORGANIZATION runs so smoothly that there is no room for complaint about it. Implicit in the reply "I can't complain" to the casual question "How are things going?" is the recognition that complaints could be made, but they are not of sufficient magnitude to warrant making them or taking action upon them. In some instances, the sentence "It wouldn't do any good anyway," appended to the reply, explicitly confirms this conclusion.

Members of Eastern City's police department reflect an "I can't complain" attitude and vary in intensity of feeling about the complaints that they cannot, or will not, make in proportion to their status or rank within the department. Patrolmen and patrolwomen are less guarded and in general are more candid about their views than are the "brass." In most areas discussed in the preceding chapters, command officers, from the top executives down to sergeants, in proportion to their rank, are highly selective in their choice of words and in the impression they wish to convey. They frequently resort to including the phrase "off the record," even when the information relayed would create little or no problem if publicized. In some cases, the information is already public knowledge.

Complaints about "too much brass" or about who gets promoted and how they obtain their promotions are most commonly heard. Experts in the field are divided in their opinions as to whether the chief executive of the police department should be selected by a civil-service examination or appointed by the mayor or city manager.[1] Some argue that the civil-service examination minimizes the political aspect and maximizes the competence aspect of the candidate's appointment. Others feel that the civil-service examination may be passed by one who is proficient in test taking but who could not manage the department or effectively serve the mayor or local government.

Eastern City's police are divided in their views of promotion in the ranks from sergeant through the chief executive officer. No one argues against civil-service examinations for the patrol rank. It has become standard throughout most of the cities in the nation that entrance to the lowest rank in the department should be through an examination. Appointment of the chief and examination for all others, except deputy or assistant chiefs, is the practice in most cities. In Eastern City all ranks above patrol are appointed.

Complaints about politics and promotion, drinking, and favoritism highlight the list of factors that are cited as causes of lowered morale. The consensus of both men and women officers is that morale is frequently low but occasionally improves. Officers in the higher positions, as might be expected, accept politics and promotion procedures as positive and normal parts of police life, while the rank-and-file members of the department express conflicting views about them. Those who have been successfully promoted think of the system as fair and just; those who think that they are in line for promotion in the near future agree with it; and those who are not politically favored within or outside of the department or who do not socialize appropriately (drinking, golfing, hunting, fishing, and so on) resent it. Exceptions to the rule are found, as in the comment of one old timer who said, "I am violently opposed to civil service. You get some bum with book knowledge who passes the exam and remains in the job he was promoted to until he is promoted again or retires." This officer likes the present system of political spoils. He has been promoted and demoted several times over the years and concluded this phase of his interview with, "I'd rather retire as a patrolman than take the exam." He still hopes for a promotion.

Although they desire promotion, there is agreement among officers in the bottom ranks that there are too many command officers from sergeant on up. As one man commented, "They've got a sergeant of paper clips and a lieutenant of library!" Officers in the higher ranks also complain. They, too, see the department as top-heavy, and with their "off the record" statements they include casual remarks about the number of their peers who should not be there, and long-contemplated ideas about their own greater capacities to serve in the higher or highest positions of the department than those of the incumbents.

"Whom you know" rather than "what you know" is a means for obtaining desired results as common in the police department as on the streets where the police grew up. The method may be used in all walks of life, but it is more intensely maintained on the policeman's side of town and on his job than elsewhere. He may resent the process, but he accepts it as fate. His acceptance creates a built-in mechanism for constant low morale for himself and the majority of his peers. Morale is temporarily improved only when his "luck" changes and "those he knows" are in political power within the community. Of course, his promotion, he knows, is due entirely to his superior qualifications (which only a political friend seems to be able to see).

The promotional policy that depends on political spoils not only has the potential for rewarding incompetent personnel (along with those who may be competent), but additionally creates among the unpromoted officers a lack of harmony or unity and a lack of will to perform to full capacity. Again, the words of a member of Eastern City's department as he contemplated the situation, best describe the predominant departmental view: "There is no incentive to be outstanding, if you can be. There are no rewards. Only you know how good you do on the job. If you foul up on the job, you'll hear about it. Nobody gets promoted without a sponsor."

It is easier to pose questions than to answer them, and it is not unusual in books reporting research to evade answers entirely.

Nevertheless, at the risk of accusations of overdistension, suggestions for possible solutions to police questions are included within the remaining pages.

There is little doubt that the officers of Eastern City are ambivalent about their own promotion policies. They have made no effort to change them; when a vote was taken, they voted against any change. Luck or skill in politicking and "lucking out" with the party in power do not, according to the police themselves, either serve as incentive to do superior work or keep morale high. Some officers may depend on luck rather than skillful police work based on effective training. The negative attitude toward training and toward education in general discussed in Chapter 2 is reinforced by the knowledge that promotion is linked only slightly to capacity to perform police work. The fact that politicians may go out of their way, on occasion, to pick the most capable candidate(s) for the job(s) in order to get the work done well and possibly indirectly enhance their own positions does not alleviate the prevailing attitude that the most incompetent get promoted.

Drinking and favoritism are aspects of the promotion picture painted above. Camaraderie among police plays a significant role in their life styles on and off the job. In chapter 3 the life styles of the "police buddy" (and the homebody) were detailed and the frequent instability of the family life of police officers revealed. Excessive drunkenness limits one's chances for promotion, but "drinking with the boys," occasionally to excess, enhances one's position. Because of shift work, "drinking with the boys" refers most often to drinking with other members of one's platoon. Morale can be described as high in such a platoon. A "police-buddy" type has said, "I think out department has the best morale in the world. We are always kidding around on our platoon. We go out together and nobody dislikes one another. It's fabulous." Another "police buddy," from another platoon, recognized that drinking with the platoon was not sufficient insurance of favor for an individual or a platoon, that favoritism went beyond the platoon. "Morale stinks," he said, "The main reason is promotion, and every captain has his favorites for that." Then he decried the lack of special privilege that friendly superiors had allowed when the laws were less clear. "It's not for the record, but things were better when we could disregard some laws. No one could call you a pig or something like that without getting beat up by you. We still do [beat up people] if no one is around—but guys coming out of the academy learn to put up with that crap."

Eastern City's police department, like any other bureaucratic organization, works best when both its executive, the command, and its rank and file, the patrol personnel, adhere to organizational principles. It is at its worst when its members undermine it by carrying over their primary-group membership into their secondary-group activities. A patrolman who drinks, hunts, fishes, or golfs with his lieutenant has no right to expect the lieutenant to maintain a *personal* relationship with him while on duty. *Informality* may prevail; "Mike" rather than "Officer Smith" could be the form of greeting; but while on duty, superordination and subordination are still paramount, and a patrolman is required *impersonally* to obey a lieutenant's command. Some men expect privilege because they do not clearly delineate the boundaries of their work, their friendships, and their home lives. Several Eastern City officers feel that they have been betrayed by their superiors because they are no longer allowed to leave their posts early to go to other jobs that they hold. Still others express annoyance that "working cars" are not sent to their homes, as in the past, to take them to and from work.

In this day and age, when images of occupations are changing, pedestals are crumbling, ministers and schoolteachers are recognized as human, and politicians in high government positions are found to have feet of clay (or mud), it might be profitable for police officers to reassess who and where they are in the social system. With less effort to maintain an exemplary image, and with a wider circle of friends, they might develop less inbred attitudes, and the tendency to create role conflicts through the overlap of friendship and occupational activities might decrease.

"There's no use complaining" and "Morale could always be better" are phrases that express resignation and the acceptance of society's attitudes toward the police, which they interpret as hostility or indifference. Though it may seem like a contradiction, since they seek and expect personal favors for their own advancement, the police do not expect help from their legislators. One policeman, as early as 1970, summed up his observation of lack of public support and combined it with his hostility for the government with the prophetic statement

> Our younger generation, including college students, have [sic] no respect for The Establishment. The police are the scapegoats for many social ills today. Irregardless of public relation, the stigma remains until society goes on to other targets. Perhaps the next scapegoats will be the politicians.

The police of Eastern City have never forgiven the U.S. Supreme Court for the decisions that upheld the right to obtain legal counsel, the right to remain silent, and other rights of alleged offenders. Aside from limiting their techniques for gathering evidence for prosecution, such decisions convinced them that the highest court in the land was as weak as the local criminal courts— which, in their eyes, cater to the criminal. The courts, they feel, do not cooperate with them. They do not convict, or if they do, they do not mete out the sentences that the officers believe should be given. This resentment might be dealt with by clearer explanations of police and court functions in college and police-academy courses. A clearer delineation of their own duties and those of the courts to the public would lessen, if not eliminate, the tension between the two.

"We are afraid that we are going to be 'put down' after an arrest," is the attitude of the police. It expresses their perception of community, court, and local government authorities' reactions to them. The accusation of overdistension of authority discussed in chapter 5 is frequently counteracted by the police by limited or no action. The refusal to act may reflect insecurity caused by lack of public support and indistinct legal boundaries, or it may be passive resistance. In effect, the officer may be saying to the public, "This is what happens when you do not permit me to use my own discretion."

But unlimited authority does not answer the police officer's dilemma. As chapter 5 shows, clearer legislation and the support of officials within the department and of legislators, rather than wider police powers, would answer the officers' needs and bolster the morale of the department.

The study of ex-convicts reported in chapter 4 reveals the ironic fact that, with regard to the police, they are among the most supportive—or at least the most understanding—groups in the community. It is not hard to see why. Although one must be careful not to overgeneralize, the officer and the criminal may come from the same side of town, may have shared experiences (possibly even playing "cops and robbers" together), and may have had contacts with more people on the "shady" side of the law than most other people growing up in their city. These experiences could very well lead to a shared perspective about police work. Basically, the ex-convicts confirm Sutherland's Theory of Differential Association.[2] *What this theory states is that support and understanding are not synonymous with acceptance.* A knowedge of their similarities and differences can lead to understanding and possibly mutual support between groups, but it does not create mutual acceptance. Obviously it does not in the case of the ex-convict and the police. Nevertheless, if ex-convicts, a group that police expect to be hostile toward them, are not, then the police perceptions of the public are faulty and reflect their own suspicious natures more than reality. Only a greater contact with the public through public relations efforts (rather than through law violations by the public) will lead to public understanding and support. Dilution of police social-class "purity" by members of other classes and of varied racial and ethnic backgrounds can act as a catalyst for understanding. Explanations of race and class differences presented in college or academy courses cannot succeed as well as personal contact. Acceptance of the police by the public (other than the ex-convicts and other deviants) could come through an awareness of the police's greater acceptance of that public. That acceptance could be forthcoming when both the police and the public see the police as people whose function is to serve the public. The present adversary system of relationships is not conducive to that end. The police act as agents of the government rather than the people. Any contact with the police by the majority of people is preceded by the stated or thought question, "What did I do wrong?" Fear dominates the attitude of the citizen approached by the police. What the citizen doesn't know is that the police harbor fear also. The fear is of the unknown response of the public which could be hostile, dangerous, or simply degrading, but which could also be pleasant and rewarding.

Most of Eastern City's police officers, with the exception of those closest to the top, do not aspire to be chief, even though they seek promotion. When asked how they would improve the department, were they to be promoted to the rank of chief, most make suggestions that would directly improve their present lot, such as a new patrol car or less paperwork. The suggestions, though sometimes contradictory, reflect that, on the whole, the critical needs of the department include education and a code of ethcs. While many responses were explicit as to the type of supplies needed, few included any elaboration about what education should consist of or what should be in the code of ethics. Only the women officers included in their list of needs of the department that there should be introduced into the department, in some way, an awareness that there is a relationship between family, friendships, and job.

There is no relationship between rank and type of suggestion made. The women officers, however, consistently suggested psychosocial or philosophical rather than material changes. Captains, lieutenants, and patrolmen alike called for new equipment and a new record system. With few exceptions, educating the police and the public about the police as people and

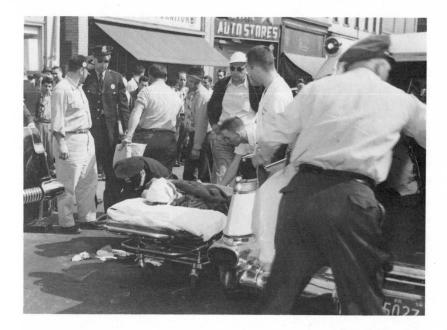

A severe accident. While one officer attempts to aid and comfort the victim, the other calmly interrogates a witness. Aiding victims and prosecuting offenders sums up the occupational lives of the police. (Bethlehem Police Dept., Bethlehem, Pa.)

their work was suggested. One officer made the astute observation about training courses that "Everytime we have a special school, it's on something we already know. I don't know much about drugs or handling people before an arrest." Morale and performance should rise when the officers become accustomed to being surveyed as to their own training needs and have a choice in course selection.

One hears, on occasion, that most of the "better" schools (courses) are attended by administrators who will neither use the knowledge in the performance of their duties nor train others who could use it. Again, consultation of the membership of the department could rectify this error, if it exists, or correct the erroneous impression that it does. If it is true that line officers, for example, should attend a particular school, then freer communication through channels would make those higher in the ranks aware of the need. If it is shown that administrators actually need the training to carry out their duties, freer communication would correct erroneous assumptions about the misuse of educational programs and raise the morale of the department.

To be misunderstood leads to depression. To misunderstand leads to inappropriate response. The police and their public are guilty of both; each, therefore, has a stake in altering both conditions. The police can be better understood at home, among their friends, and within their communities through greater openness on their part and a decrease in their assumed need to appear big, tough, and model citizens when off duty. (Certainly their interacting exclusively with each other does not foster understanding by the wider society.) They can decrease their own misperceptions by being slower in reaching conclusions about those that they assume to know and through clearer directives from superiors as to the extent and limitations of their duties. The public will react to whatever image the police project. They are less likely than the police to make a concerted effort to understand. Those who do wish to begin such an undertaking, to understand the lot of the police as occupationals on the firing line of the community, have started the task with the glimpses into police life contained in this book.

Notes

1. Caldwell, Robert G., *Criminology,* 2d ed. (New York: The Ronald Press, 1965), pp. 294-295.

2. Sutherland, Edwin H., and Cressey, Donald, *Criminology,* 9th ed. (Philadelphia: J. B. Lippincott, 1974), Chapter 4.

BIBLIOGRAPHY

Baldwin, Roger. "The Police and the Ex-Convict." *Criminology* 8 (1970).

Baldwin, Roger. "Reciprocal Suspicion: Side One." In *Crime, Prevention, and Social Control,* edited by Edward Sagarin and Ronald Akers. New York: Praeger, 1974.

Barocas, Harvey. "Iatrogenic and Preventive Intervention in Police Family Crisis Situations." American Society of Criminology, Inter-American Conference, Caracas, Venezuela, November, 1972.

Bayley, David H., and Mendelsohn, Harold. *Minorities and the Police: Confrontation in America.* New York: The Free Press, 1969.

Bierstedt, Robert. "The Problem of Authority." In *The Study of Society,* edited by Peter I. Rose. New York: Random House, 1967.

Bierstedt, Robert. *The Social Order.* 3d ed. New York: McGraw-Hill, 1970.

Bittner, E. "The Police on Skid-Row: A Study of Peace Keeping." In *Crime and the Legal Process,* edited by W. Chamblis. New York: McGraw-Hill, 1968.

Brown, Lee P. "The Police in Higher Education: The Challenge of the Times." *Criminology* 12 (1974).

Caldwell, Robert G. *Criminology.* 2d ed. New York: The Ronald Press, 1965.

Cloward, Richard, and Ohlin, Lloyd E. *Delinquency and Opportunity.* Glencoe, Ill.: The Free Press, 1961.

Etzioni, Amitai. *Modern Organizations.* Englewood Cliffs, N.J.: Prentice-Hall, 1964.

Fosdick, Raymond B. *American Police Systems.* New York: The Century Co., 1921.

Gamire, Bernard I., Rubin, Jesse, and Wilson, James Q. *The Police and the Community.* Baltimore: Johns Hopkins University Press, 1972.

Gans, Herbert. *The Levittowners.* New York: Pantheon Books, 1967.

Kinsey, Alfred C., Pomeroy, Wardell B., and Martin, Clyde E. *Sexual Behavior in the Human Male.* Philadelphia: W. B. Saunders, 1948.

Kinsey, Alfred C., Pomeroy, Wardell B., and Martin, Clyde E. *Sexual Behavior in the Human Female.* Philadelphia: W. B. Saunders, 1953.

Kirkham, George L. "The Female Homosexual." In *Critical Issues in the Study of Crime,* edited by Simon Dinitz and Walter C. Reckless. Boston: Little, Brown and Co., 1969.

Komarovsky, Mirra. *Blue Collar Marriage.* New York: Random House, 1962.

Laing, D., Phillipson, H., and Lee, A. R. *Interpersonal Perception.* New York: Springer Publishing Co., 1966.

Law Enforcement Assistance Administration. *Operation Demonstration.* U.S. Department of Justice, 1975.

LeMasters, E. E. *Parents in Modern America.* Rev. ed. Homewood, Ill.: Dorsey Press, 1974.

Lemert, Edwin M. "Prostitution." In *Problems of Sex Behavior,* edited by Edward Sagarin and Donal E. F. MacNamara. New York: Thomas Y. Crowell Co., 1968.

MacIver, Robert M. *Society: A Textbook of Sociology.* New York: Farrar and Rinehart, 1937.

McCaghy, Charles H. "Child Molesters: A Study of Their Careers as Deviants." In *Criminal Behavior Systems, A Typology,* edited by Marshall D. Clinard and Richard Quinney. New York: Holt, Rinehart and Winston, 1967.

McNamara, John H. "Uncertainties in Police Work: The Relevance of Police Recruits Background and Training." In *The Police, Six Sociological Essays,* edited by David J. Bordua. New York: John Wiley, 1967.

Morris, Norval. "Politics and Pragmatism in Crime Control." *Federal Probation,* June 1968.

National Advisory Commission on Criminal Justice Standards and and Goals, *Executive Summary.* Washington, D.C.: U.S. Department of Justice, 1973.

Newman, Donald J. *Introduction to Criminal Justice.* Philadelphia: J. B. Lippincott, 1975.

Niederhoffer, Arthur. *Behind the Shield: The Police in Urban Society.* Garden City, N.Y.: Doubleday, 1967.

Packer, Herbert L. "The Two Models of the Criminal Process." *University of Pennsylvania Law Review* 113 (1964).

Packer, Herbert L. *The Limits of the Criminal Sanction.* Stanford, Calif.: Stanford University Press, 1968.

Reiss, Albert J., Jr. *The Police and the Public.* New Haven: Yale University Press, 1971.

Reiss, Ira L. *The Social Context of Premarital Sexual Permissiveness.* New York: Holt, Rinehart and Winston, 1967.

Rubinstein, Jonathan. "From the King's Peace to the Patrol Car: The Origins of the City Police." *New York,* May 14, 1973.

Sagarin, Edward. "Invitation to an Invasion: Some Reflections on the Invasion of Privacy." *Criminologica* 5 (1967).

Sagarin, Edward. *The Other Minorities.* New York: Ginn and Co., 1971.

Schafer, Stephen. *The Victim and His Criminal.* New York: Random House, 1968.

Schur, Edwin. *Crimes without Victims.* Englewood Cliffs, N.J.: Prentice-Hall, 1965.

Skolnick, Jerome H. *Justice without Trial.* New York: John Wiley and Sons, 1967.

Skolnick, Jerome H. "Why Police Behave the Way They Do." In *Police in America,* edited by Jerome Skolnick and Thomas Gray. Boston: Educational Associates, 1975.

Skolnick, Jerome H., and Woodworth, J. Richard. "Bureaucracy, Information, and Social Control: A Study of a Morals Detail." In *The Police: Six Sociological Essays,* edited by David Bordua. New York: John Wiley and Sons, 1967.

Stern, Mort. "What Makes a Policeman Go Wrong." In *The Ambivalent Force,* edited by Arthur Niederhoffer and Abraham Blumberg. Waltham, Mass.: Ginn and Co., 1970.

Sutherland, Edwin, and Cressey, Donald. *Criminology.* 9th ed. Philadelphia: Lippincott, 1972.

Sweet, Robert E. "Seattle Police Wives Learning About Husbands' Jobs." *Allentown* (Pa.) *Sunday Call-Chronicle,* June 13, 1971.

Terris, Bruce J. "The Role of the Police." *The Annals* 374 (1967).

Tiffany, Lawrence P., McIntyre, Donald M., and Rotenberg, Daniel L. *Detection of Crime.* Boston: Little, Brown and Co., 1967.

Uniform Crime Reports, 1973.

Uniform Crime Reports, 1974.

Vidich, Arthur, and Bensman, Joseph. *Small Town in Mass Society.* Princeton, N.J.: Princeton University Press, 1969.

Waldron, Ronald J., Uppa, Jagdish C., Quarles, Chester L., McCauley, R. Paul, Harper, Hilary, Frazier, Robert L., Benson, James C., and Altemose, John R. *The Criminal Justice System: An Introduction.* Boston: Houghton Mifflin, 1976.

Westley. "Violence and the Police." In *Crime and the Legal Process,* edited by W. Chamblis. New York: McGraw-Hill, 1968.

Wilson, J. Q. "Police Morale, Reform, and Citizen Respect: The Chicago Case." In *The Police: Six Sociological Essays,* edited by David Bordua. New York: John Wiley, 1967.

Winslow, R. W., ed. *Crime in a Free Society: Selections from the President's Commission on Law Enforcement and Administration of Justice.* Belmont, Calif.: Dickinson Publishing, 1968.

Wolff, Kurt H., ed. *The Sociology of Georg Simmel.* New York: The Free Press, 1950.

Wood, Robert C. *Suburbia.* Boston: Houghton Mifflin, 1959.

Wrong, Dennis. "Some Problems in Defining Social Power." *American Journal of Sociology* 73 (1968).

INDEX